Each of You
A Spiritual Journey Shifting from Darkness to Light

James Nussbaumer

For permission, serialization, condensation, adaptions, or for our catalog of other publications, write to Ozark Mountain Publishing, Inc., P.O. Box 754, Huntsville, AR 72740, ATTN: Permissions Department.

Library of Congress Cataloging-in-Publication Data

Each of You by James Nussbaumer -1957-

You have the divine power to escape darkness in your life and allow this Heavenly Light to guide you on an uplifting Journey through Life in this world.

1. Divine 2. Spiritual 3. Forgiveness 4. Purpose

I. Nussbaumer, James, 1957 II. Divine   III. Spiritual   IV. Title

Library of Congress Catalog Card Number: 2022942875

ISBN: 9781956945225

Cover Art and Layout: Victoria Cooper Art
Book set in: Multiple Fonts
Book Design: Summer Garr
Published by:

PO Box 754, Huntsville, AR 72740

800-935-0045 or 479-738-2348; fax 479-738-2448

WWW.OZARKMT.COM

Printed in the United States of America

I dedicate this book to all our sons and daughters, and to all of us, too, who might seem lost.

Let us remember that it is quite possible to listen to God's Voice all through the day without interrupting your regular activities in any way. You will come to realize the part of you that is listening to the Voice for God is calm, always at rest, and wholly certain.

"Conformity is the jailer of freedom and the enemy of growth. We need men and women who can dream of things that never were."

—President John F. Kennedy

Contents

Part I

Uncovering the Light of Wholeness

Chapter 1

Introduction: Our Psychological Self

When I began the outline for this book, I knew the message I wanted to get across, but didn't know how to deliver it. A familiar urge inside of me began to ramble with a rhythm that made sense to me. So I proceeded to ramble while feeling a hint of guilt due to being taught that an outline is not the place for that. So I let go of the idea of needing an outline and just began writing.

For those of you who know me personally who might be sarcastically but lovingly saying to yourself, "You, Jim Nussbaumer, ramble on? Hard to believe!" the rambling result is now being held in your hands. Please read on and find out if it's truly hard to believe.

* * *

I'd always been intrigued by time and how it moves people to meet one another, how it sets up events making history and the lives we lead. I am convinced and so may you be, that where we've come and how we've arrived as well as where we are now is not only coincidence.

I've often wondered, where was the mind of individuals like Henry Ford, Thomas Edison, Ben Franklin, and the other Founding Fathers, only to mention a few, in relation to how we think and do things today? Or, let's consider even earlier back in time to Shakespeare, Davinci, Newton, Galileo, and the like, and further to the prehistoric cave men and women. What is it that separates us today from all of history?

Did they really exist in history or is it only in our minds that reflect their existence? I know, here I go again, rambling on and may seem to not be making sense. We'll touch on that thought ahead in this book. So please hang on.

But overall, in my mind I'd have to say based on my own experiences, what actually separates us turns out to be psychology. With Freud having come along onto the scene, the psychological climate of this world changed and our self-reflective generation is what we have today. But I'll admit, at first thought I was going to say technology and its innovations as the most separating aspect. But certainly, psychology has fueled the furnace.

What's really difficult for me to comprehend is the pre-Freudian way of processing reality. The way people lived off their land, in a one-room log cabin or soddie with only a small fireplace for warmth and cooking. Not to forget the shortened life spans due to limited health awareness and psychological awareness.

For me as a child growing up in the 1960s, technology meant the twenty-four-inch Admiral, black-and-white television set, until finally the Zenith color TV found its way into our family's living room just in time for the first moon walk. This was at a time when parents did not understand their teenagers, some adults were afraid of them, and flower power was streaking across the country. Now our parents are old and so are we, and their experiences led them to different conclusions about the world. It's a conclusion that keeps us from reaching them to the root of who they are.

Many of the tensions between the generations have never been personal. The difficulties are nobody's fault. We can't change our histories, but we can change how we look at them. I mean changing our minds about what the past represents.

Our futures can be shaped more positively if we can become more aware that surface-structure differences don't always reflect differences in deep-structure motivations. We need translations and reinterpretations rather than conflict that lead to war and the threat of world annihilation. Regardless of any generation gap, we learn from one another whether we realize it or not.

* * *

Think about when the study of psychology came to the different areas of this world. In America, psychology greatly influenced urban sophisticates and intellects in the 1910s and 1920s, but most Americans knew nothing about it when World War II came about. The Midwest was slower to catch on than the East Coast, and since many writers were heavily influenced by Freud, readers were familiar with psychology sooner than nonreaders.

When I graduated from Central Catholic in 1975, I'd never heard of psychotherapy. Now it's everywhere. Pre-teens today talk about being "in the zone." Small-town folks talk about low self-esteem, depression, panic disorders, and Freudian slips. Truck drivers go to therapists and hairstylists analyze their customers' dreams. My ex-wife, Lori, is good at that. Golf professionals seek to go deeper within their game wanting to see something on the putting green they've been missing, something deeper than which direction the turf is growing.

As progress propels us, people seem to want to go back to the basics, but in a more sophisticated fashion. My friend Ollie Hendrix goes fishing alone to relieve stress and get in tune with himself. He uses the same old-fashioned jig for bait, but also uses the latest high-tech fish finder, attached to his boat. Is this a good example? It might not be for you, but ask Ollie how it feels when later that day he goes home with a stringer full of crappie. Dinner on the table.

Many issues such as alcoholism, once denied or thought of as sinful, are now considered mental health issues. Instead of the old, "I'm okay, you're okay," we've become the "I'm dysfunctional, you're dysfunctional" culture. Some may use the excuse, "I come from a dysfunctional family." But tell me, what family is functional? People who laugh all the time and cut up are often viewed as in denial or hypocritical.

If you say you've had a happy childhood, you are less likely to be believed than if you say that you were traumatized or abused by cruel parents. We no longer believe that there are well-adjusted people, but we can see those who are skilled at masking their pathologies. We now live in an upside-down model for mental health, where the sick are well and vice versa. We trust the miserable and questionable and we doubt those who are perky with certainty.

Today, popular psychology is on radio and TV talk shows, in women's and men's magazines, sports magazines, presidential and other political speeches. Perception, *thinking for change*, and projection are household words. There is a cartoon I recently saw in a magazine, where a doorman for an apartment building says to a little girl, "Your mother must have a hidden agenda, the way she gave you those extra cookies." My friend Mike Hofacker has said, "We golfing maniacs seem obsessed with taking our emotional temperature when we end a good or a bad round of golf." Hofy has often been known to pose as a clinical psychologist at the nineteenth hole if needing an ear to bend.

For many people today, therapy is in our blood and is the answer to everything. I think of modern-day author Harlan Coben, who said on a TV interview, "We keep thinking we're still age seventeen, waiting for life to begin."

Turn the page and relax as we explore how you can begin realizing that real life and real relationships are here with you, *now.*

Chapter 2

Your Limited Existence

Humankind seems to be constantly confronted with loss and suffering, and we tend to think this is the meaning of life. As people move on in life while we're getting older ourselves, we understand there will never be anyone like who we've lost, ever again. We try hard to make relationships lasting. When relationships end for whatever reason, especially in death, it often helps us to see what is important. What is unimportant recedes into shadows.

As we age and grow we need wisdom, philosophy, psychology, poetry, art, music, and a sense of being connected to something meaningful. Our lives, then, become more *sacred* and *holy*, as I would define the words. To me, *sacred* is that which moves toward wholeness. I've accepted *holiness* to be certain resilience, growing from experience and becoming more of who one truly is. In my mind those that are *holy* seem to live with a purpose that results in a glow about them.

A major purpose we have as we experience life is the realization of what is real versus the unreal, or the growing of spirit. Spirit, in the context I use it, is synonymous with character. We can say it is the governor of one's thought system, along with the faith that motivates and explains every action. The spirit in us is that which endures and which gives us meaning. When I write about the spirit, I think of those who have been lifelong learners, where their whole life has been about growing and nurturing their spirit while extending joy from that.

* * *

Regardless of the self-help books you've read that are piled in the corner of the spare bedroom you may call your library, or the seminars for success you've attended, or the personal power meditations you practice consistently, which are all good, you still feel your life is limited. You're not alone in this feeling. But I sincerely applaud you for being on the positive path.

You've seen a loved one lose the battle to something like cancer, or maybe you are currently involved in a similar battle yourself. Or, maybe it's your career you see as a dead end, or you are jobless, getting a divorce, or whatever pain it might be, you see a limit to yourself and life.

Why is this?

There will always be limits on ourselves no matter how positive we think we might be, as long as our awareness is of the body. The body is seen as your limit on life. The belief in a limited life is how your body came into this world. The belief in a limited life is how your world evolves. Somewhere, before your physical form was seen in this world, you decided on limits to the unlimited. That thought and others like it are separation from the *unlimited or true reality.* This projection of life is how we got here in bodily form. We'll be going into this later.

But for now, try to see that humankind has done this to himself and continues to think the body is separate from but still a symbolic representation of Divinity. As yourself, when you see yourself as a body can you also see yourself as an idea? In other words, are you a bodily form or are you an idea?

An idea in itself is within your spirit and can be shared, but it is not form. All form you recognize is identified as outside yourself, shapes, sizes, and structures that mingle among one another, or something imaginable. Think about it. Isn't it even difficult to think about God without the thoughts of an old man with a white beard in a white robe sitting on a golden throne, a body? We liked the image George Burns gave us of God, in the movie. We like to project an image of God in a similar form we'd recognize.

Many of us believe in the existence of body, mind, and spirit.

8

The balance of all three seems to be important to our philosophy. But you will soon learn, rather than your seemingly separated mind that makes and uses bodies, that you must choose between the limited and the unlimited eternal reality of spirit. Your choice is the wholeness that you truly are—or the unreal and ever-changing universe of bodies—which includes anything that can be perceived, whether you appear to be in a body or not. You cannot be partly whole. This state of mind doesn't come to you all at once. Nothing worthwhile is learned overnight.

Your body cannot relate with or know God. You will never see the grandeur that surrounds you while you limit your awareness or yourself to the body and its senses. God is not in your body, nor can you join Him there.

You've been seeing yourself as separate or apart from God because of your beliefs in limits. This shuts Him out, meaning your body cannot be of God. Your limits on yourself have separated you from the unlimited. Wouldn't you agree that if you are limited, you can never be within the unlimited? Ask yourself, is your true reality limited?

Chapter 3

The Fence for Guilt

Not sex nor nudity, but *guilt* is the biggest secret ever, and it must be looked at to overcome its fear. My friend Fran once told me of needing to change her father's diapers; he was a stroke victim. He was humiliated and apologetic let alone in tears. She told him, "Please, Dad, you once changed many of my diapers. Now it's my turn."

You may experience guilt in many issues even when you've wondered why. Have you ever asked yourself: "Why am I feeling guilty about this?"

Your choice to separate yourself from the unlimited is the guilt-plagued issue that puts a limit on you. This haunts the limited aspect about you. You have made your body to be like a tiny fence that surrounds a little part of a glorious and complete idea.

Try to imagine drawing a small crack inside a very large segment of Heaven. The fence is your body. A tiny part of your mind thinks it has split itself away from the whole of life eternal, which is Heaven, and you are projecting an image of you as this body as a barrier or fence to hide your guilt—and you call this life.

You proclaim that within this fence is your kingdom, but you've limited not only yourself, but God, too. Even if you allow God to enter, you will have limited Him by your fence. This is why you project God as being located "out there." You see everyone else with their own little fences making them separate from God, too. Can you just imagine Saint Peter busy finding places, walking around with a clipboard, inside of Heaven trying to make room for all these fences?

That may sound a bit crazy and it is intended to, because isn't this the illusion many of us live by? "Reserving one's spot in Heaven" seems to be a goal in life for those who fear their destiny. Let's look more deeply at this.

This limiting thought system which must be separate from God because He has no limits, cruelly rules the boundaries of your fence. At best, it is an ultimate speck of dust you wish to defend against the universe. The decidedly separated and split tiny piece of mind fragments itself continually while it projects images of other bodies along with your own all-hiding guilt. It's only an elusive thought, comparable to a dream or a daze of sort, and such a nonexistent part of the *real* universe—that would be similar to a sunray having an existence separate from the sun. Or, could you imagine the faintest ripple of ocean water, alone and separate from the ocean?

With such a lofty and grandiose attitude, this tiny sunray declares a life without being connected to or as one with the sun. Likewise, the imperceptible and unnoticeable ripple hails itself needing no power from the ocean. Does this make any sense that a droplet of ocean water would not be the ocean?

If you see your body illusively powerful as this, no wonder you are frightened and often frustrated in your thoughts of life, and why you fear death. You may say you believe in God, it's what you were taught, but you still maintain that you are *separate* from Him.

This is why we hide our guilt and often try desperately to hide or shy away from the truth. The truth about what? you might ask. About everything and anything. Even the truth about your uncertainty of what the truth actually is. How about the truth in the fact that we conjure up what we'd like to be the truth, in order to make ourselves appear to not be afraid of our own shadow? Or, perhaps the truth in the fact we know the truth, but fear facing it? What about the truth that you as well as God are not truly a body? Why would this scare us?

As we move through this book together you will gradually

come to realize the truth that there is no real death and that your real relationships are eternal. Yes, I mean they last forever.

Your limited and separate thoughts from your Source have made an image of death only because deep within, you want to put an end to this *limitation business*. But because you made the body, your separate-minded self—your ego—will not let go of the bodily image as being who you are. You will learn as we continue that *ego* in this sense is *not* indicating "egotistical," but the ego-based mind in its definition of separateness surely is the breeding ground for egotistical behavior. The ego-based mind is the elusive thought system you fear losing a grip on. Why? It's what sees the body.

Think for a moment how you see the complete universe outside yourself, not understanding it and afraid of its uncertainty, no different from the sunray seeing the sun far off and separate from itself. In the same sense the ocean terrifies the ripple as though it wants to swallow it. Nothing real can have power without its source.

* * *

Consider the source of electricity in your home, say, the power company. Is this company aware when a circuit breaker trips in the breaker box located in your home? A source is not aware of strange and separate activity while it simply continues its function, unaware that it is feared and hated by a tiny segment of itself that dreams it is separate. Is the sun aware that clouds move in to block its light on a particular area of the earth? Whatever the tiny segment illusively thinks it is, in no way changes its true dependence on its source for true existence. Its whole real existence truly remains unseparated, otherwise the sunray, for example, would be gone; the ripple of water inconceivable without its ocean.

It's the same strange projection of images which those in a world of bodies *seem* to be. Each body seems to house a separate mind, but living alone and in no way joined to the Thought of Who created it. Each tiny fragment of thought seems to be self-contained, limited; needing another for something regarding its own survival, but by no means sees itself as totally dependent on its creator for everything.

Being split apart, fragmented and separate from its source, how can this illusive thought system have a real source? It can't, so it doesn't.

Everything is of fantasy in the ego-based thought system. Illusion is its source. It makes up its source as it goes along and to its liking. This is why its entire thought pattern is unreal because its source is unreal, filled with limits of what this system can do and cannot do. It has a fantasy of not needing the whole of life to give it any meaning and by itself it means nothing.

But just like the sun and the ocean, our true and real whole self continues unmindful that this tiny fenced-off area thinks of it split away and guarded. Regardless of the fence, this area does not exist only with its real *Source*, nor would the whole of life be whole without you. You are not a separate kingdom ruled by an errant thought of being separate from the rest.

There really is no fence that surrounds your kingdom, preventing you from joining with the rest of Heaven and keeping you separate from your Creator. He did not create you outside of Himself; you have always been within His mind. The fenced-off area you think you are leads no separate life, it just thinks it does. What is eternal other than all that exists within the mind of God? There can be nothing real outside of true oneness. Don't you agree?

Chapter 4

Transformation

Are you accepting this tiny little fence and its enclosed area as yourself, alone? The sun and ocean do not compare to what you truly are. The sun's little ray is bright only in the light of the sun, and the ripple dances only as the ocean roars. Yet neither the sun nor ocean has the power that abides in you.

You will be discovering in the pages ahead why your real relationships are not bound within this fence you claim as your tiny kingdom. What will come forward in your mind will keep you from remaining a worrisome king, a guilty ruler of all that you project, affecting your relationships, looking on fantasy as being important while defending your fear of dying.

You will grow with each line in these pages to exceed the little self or little fence that is *not* really you. Deep within you and surrounding this reality, infinitely with love, beyond what this world has taught you, is the glorious wholeness of life. It welcomes you as part of its happiness and deep context. This little external appearance from your body's eyesight that you thought sets you apart, is no exception.

You will see for yourself instead of just reading about it, that real life has no knowledge of human bodies and it reaches to everything created like it. Its limitless *is* its meaning. Real life has no body. Your reality is completely impartial in its giving because whatever is whole is contained completely within itself. Because nothing real is outside of your mind, your tiny kingdom means nothing. You'll learn to make the decision to call on life to enter as you lay down the thought of a fence as your guard or barrier.

* * *

Let's consider for a moment, the driest desert imaginable, unproductive, scorched, and joyless, which makes up what you call your tiny kingdom. Try to realize the joy and contentment that an abundant life of love would bring to it from where it comes, to where it would return within you.

Now enters the one single whole Thought of Life—God, encompassing your little kingdom, waiting at the fence you made to come inside and shine upon the barren ground. The illusive thought of the fence fades away, life suddenly springs up everywhere. The desert becomes a garden, green, lush, and deep and quiet, offering rest to those who lost their way and wander in the dust. You give them a place of refuge, prepared by love for them where a desert once was.

Everyone you welcome will bring life and love from Heaven for you. This may sound fictitious and too good to be true at this point in the book, but as you begin advancing from chapter to chapter you will come to understand it as real. They will enter one by one into this *holy* place, but they will not depart as they arrived, alone. The love of life they bring with them will stay with them just as it will stay with you. A brotherhood of whole and lasting life. How so? you ask.

You share the same mind—the fenceless garden that is no longer little. It benefits by expanding through extension and will reach deeply within everyone who thirsts for the water of the one Thought of Life that is held within His mind. No one will go on alone.

You will open your real vision to the gift of willingness and a readiness to become whole with the reality you see in others. This reality is your shared brotherhood—your brothers/sisters that you will welcome because they bring your real self to completion with them. You will grow and stretch across the desert, leaving no lonely kingdom fenced off from reality. You will recognize your real self and see your little garden transformed into the kingdom known as Heaven, with the life your creator intended for you within Him—His mind.

Your presence with eternity, that immediate proximity you always have available in a place of *no-time* and *no-space*—that instant perceptible between past and future, called the *now*. In this place is your invitation for real life to enter your bleak and joyless tiny kingdom. It will be transformed into a garden of peace and a fulfilling life. It is the real answer to life inevitable as you arrive without a body and interpose no barriers that interfere with its glad arrival.

* * *

The immediate presence of this life contains nothing more or less than an instant, an eternal *holy instant* where you ask of life only what it offers the whole, which is everything. You will receive what you ask for and it is certain. The *asking* is your self-lifting the tiny appearance that you make of yourself without Heaven's help. The kingdom will be yours like it always has been, but you didn't realize so. No part of life calls on the whole in vain or for lack of substance, where no Son of God remains outside of His Kingdom, or, we can call it His Fatherhood.

You may not have been recognizing that life has come to you, that doors have always been open. You have missed this vision because you have not let go of all the barriers you hold against being whole. What kind of barrier? you may ask. Fear for starters. Fear of what? you ask, again.

For now I'll simply add that you and your brother/sister of wholeness in mind cannot give life an open welcome separately. To even try only piles on more guilt, which means further fragmenting of the separated mind.

This means you can no more know God alone than He knows you without your brother/sister. The wholeness of each of you, those no longer here, and those yet to arrive in bodily form, have always been His whole Son. Thereby, together you are no more unaware of real life than it cannot know of you or fail to recognize in you.

Even though we appear to be in this world of form, we've already reached the end of an ancient journey, not yet realizing it is over. You are still questionable, worn, tired, and the desert's dust still seems to cloud your real vision, keeping you sightless for the time being.

My hope is that as you turn each page in this book you will begin to closely see that the fence, the desert, and all your pain have been a dream of separation from the Mind of God.

Chapter 5

Wholeness Waits for You

Many of us become overwhelmed by events that we only think shake who we are to the core. Hemingway wrote, "The worst death is the loss of what formed one's center." We only seem to lose what formed our centers. This seeming loss of one's reality projects a sense of lack.

When I entered prison and made it through the first couple of nights, I felt I was dead inside. I'd lay awake and worry about family members and friends. Would I ever see them again?

I was in a grief hangover and wishing I could put myself out of my misery. The feeling I can remember reminds me of a passage from Mark Twain's autobiography. He'd returned from Europe to hear that his daughter had died suddenly. He wrote that he felt as if a lightning bolt passed through his body and he wondered about his own physical survival.

Carl Jung believed that if we didn't develop inner strength, we'd become defensive, dogmatic, depressed, and cynical. What is most healing for people is the knowledge they are still loved, needed, and capable of loving. The ability to turn suffering into a gift for others, what Mary Pipher in her book *Another Country* called a "survivor mission," also helps us heal from loss.

Relationships mean everything to us. I am fortunate to have a few comfortably close friends, and a few of them it seems have been in my life forever. They are so important to me that I have dedicated this book to each one of them. It's not necessary that I mention their names because they already know who they are.

My friends hold our relationships in highest regard and great trust. They view our times together as I do, as exceedingly important occasions. We talk, we think of one another. We share and we evaluate our decisions. We help each other with our struggles. We respect one another's beliefs.

We are available and we're in touch. Our goal is to strengthen and help one another wherever we can. By being accountable and alert in our times together, we're effortlessly willing and able to get to the heart of any issue without the standard smoke screens and fog that frequently cloud friendships. I rather suspect that they would have appreciated my help had some comparable circumstance to my dark times of prison occurred with them, as they've helped me with my burden. Although few will I never be able to fully repay, their warm hearts and listening minds are priceless, and just their being available made all the difference in the world.

In relationships that begin to breakdown, psychologically the "symptom stage" takes an unusual setting. We notice first an alteration in routine. The person no longer calls or comes around; you just seem to lose touch. Or when he or she does come around, they are strained for words; feelings seem unnatural; you experience awkwardness, lack of eye contact, a desire to leave. The sense of humor is decidedly absent. Things simply don't seem right. "Something is wrong," we whisper to ourselves. Then we churn.

Deep down within, our spirits seem to be at a distance, a space exists that once was not there. By the way, the more sensitive you are toward people, the quicker you detect such symptoms. You feel bad "vibes" as you encounter one another. But this does not only include relationships with individuals. We have situations, events, circumstances, belief systems, projects, etc., where we've given ourselves, and this, too, is a relationship.

* * *

Whenever I finish a writing project of this magnitude, I feel a sense of sadness—and surely that was the case in the project before this one that you now enjoy. But this is also why I've committed myself to it. I slowly brought the pen to paper on this project, a sense of encouragement and inspiration urged me to keep progressing with an excitement as to where it would take me. How would this book end? What will get me there? These types of inspiring thoughts created this book.

The sadness of leaving my previous book faded and the accomplishment of its satisfying, extending message moved me here to where I am now, writing these beginning chapters. It's a peaceful and blissful state of mind.

Peace without faith will never come forward in your mind, because what you've dedicated to truth is brought there by faith. There have been some not-so-pretty paths I'd taken to discover this. You see, I've learned that faith is encompassed by everyone involved in a situation that is perceived as meaningful and whole.

What is it I really mean by "whole?"

For now, let's look at wholeness as perceiving yourself without the barrier, or, the "fence," and by overlooking it by looking beyond to your reality.

The fence analogy I've used is not intended for us to dwell on, but to simply notice it as only an illusive barrier. What I mean is, see your body for what it is to you, but don't see it as restricting you from a sense of freedom. Simply place yourself in a nonrestricted mode, allow your true feelings to occur, and the rest will come along naturally as we move on.

Every situation perceived wholeheartedly is positive and becomes an opportunity to heal your separated mind. Faith does this because in faith you have given yourself, or accepted yourself as being whole. This wholeness is about you and is the spirit of God, which is holy, so we shall name *It* his *Holy Spirit*.

When you picked up this book and began to read it, you decided to let go of every demand the ego-based mind has placed on you. This "letting go" is crucial and is what saddened me temporarily when I completed my last writing project. That discomfort was due to the change my ego saw me going through, and on to something real and new, not really new at all, but it frightened my ego-based thought system. The ego thrives impatiently that I may expose the guilt. It feels being dragged along by my real self and the thought of losing control over my body is its worry and fear. But always keep in mind the ego is not intentionally bad, it's just afraid to be complete because it can never understand through wholeness.

I must excitedly add that when I do *let go* and actually move on, as I am doing now with this new book, all that is real in my previous projects are still extending everywhere. I feel the warmth of a freedom so powerful because I'm sharing it as one with the Holy Spirit, who through wholeness extends everywhere reality exists.

For those of you who may lean toward atheism, feel free to substitute the word *wholeness* for God. The feelings I have as I write these words come from wholeness and I choose to call it God. It certainly is not separateness. Since the Holy Spirit is the spirit of the wholeness of God, He shares it with me as a gift, and this freedom is a good explanation and definition of healing.

What really is the Holy Spirit's purpose and what do I mean by a separated mind?

In my first book, *The Master of Everything*, I have "blue printed" the answer to this question, which I urge you to read and study if need be. You will discover this works in your relationships. I can tell you now that any separate-mindedness of my own is *not* the Inspiration which *caused* me to move on, let go of the past, and write this book, along with seeing my purpose real and beneficial to others in this world. My involvement here is a joining rather than a separation, and there is nothing in between. To join is to heal.

* * *

The body and its brain control our feeling of lack and that is where any feelings of despair come from, and the body cannot heal itself alone. Think about it, the body doesn't make itself sick. Its condition depends entirely on how the mind perceives it and the purpose the mind would use the brain for.

You'll learn to feel the ego in yourself as a tiny unreal

segment of the whole mind, which sees itself separate from the wholeness you feel at times of completeness. The wholeness is the *Universal Purpose* which is the *Divine Power* in each of us, but only through and wholly of each other.

When you are feeling whole, the ego will use the body as a weapon for defense against this purpose. It demonstrates its misery in the fact of being separate with its chosen thought system that can never locate solid, truthful answers. The ego-based mind uses its thought system trying desperately to drive the body. You'll notice this in the judgments you make of others and of yourself.

The body becomes dictated by illusion and fantasy, always thinking rather than *being*, and it thrives to form an identity and acts accordingly. But it is no match for how the Holy Spirit uses the body. With the ego, you actually see what is not really there and hear what Truth never said. You believe in a manner that keeps you uncertain, and this alone can be unnerving. We can say it's like being in prison. And I'll vouch for that.

Lack of faith in ourselves leads straight to illusion and its way of thinking. What is illusion? I hear you asking. It's what you project as images from your separated state of mind, rather than your capability of reflecting from the light of inner truth.

Having no faith gives you projections of others as only being a body, and the body cannot solely be used for real, loving relationships. If you do see another as a body, you have made a condition in which a true relationship will become impossible. You lack faith in yourself, and this lack you share with another is what keeps you separated from true reality.

Here's what you've done:

You have opposed the *Universal Purpose* and placed illusion of a body to stand between you and him or her and your real purpose in life. You have allowed illusion or fantasy to have priority. But even your *unreal* relationships made of illusion and fantasy rather than reflecting truth, still have something to teach you. There is a hidden ingredient that will shift you to real vision, so hope is always alive.

It surely cannot be difficult to realize that faith must be the opposite of no-faith. This faithlessness will always limit and attack, where faith will remove limitations and make whole.

Having no-faith destroys and separates, where faith will join, and this is healing. You have then given yourself freedom from the past. Now you are ready to move forward and acknowledge your reality by learning why union in relationships that are real are everywhere, and they wait for you.

Chapter 6

The Dream of Form: Our Histories

In that instant it seemed like I didn't breathe or speak or think, time had stopped, with a certainty of what I needed to do next. The other three players, close friends, were already in the cup on this 410-yard par four, eighteenth, slick as glass, putting surface. A successful putt would win the match with bragging rights reserved for the warmth of the *Sand Trap Lounge*, afterward, where all wagers would be settled. A tradition for this grizzly foursome.

I stepped up to evaluate the seven-and-a-half-foot task in front of me. A steady plumb bob with my left eye, confidently perceived the line presenting itself vividly, as if it had been inscribed across the dance floor in incandescent paint, and as if a trough to the hole was waiting for a delicate stroke.

I stood over the ball with my feet firmly spiked into the turf, the blade of my putter was perfectly square at impact and the ball rolled in. A downhill left-to-right slider, struck not too hard and not too soft, taking the five-inch break and entering the cup on the edge. It was side door all the way to tumble and rattle heart-stopping in the bottom of the cup. It seemed to happen in slow motion.

My brain was functioning entirely from its stem and no higher. It wasn't until a half hour later where the four of us were already secure at a corner table next to the old stone fireplace in this bitter cold Ohio October afternoon. We talked up the scorecards while I returned to myself. That golf round was waiting to be recapped over a few foaming pitchers of cold beer among the camaraderie we offered one another, and reminiscing the day is how we each accepted it.

I played the final eighteen of thirty-six holes in seventy-four strokes including two balls forever lost in the woods. The fact of this gut match was complete for the day as we each grasped the moment for a friendship never to die. A brotherhood. A toast or two of cheer sealed the day as a page or two in our own little history book, then each of us returned to our own reality and headed for home.

* * *

It seems that history is what makes us and the world around us, which has been shaped over only what seems to be millions of years to that point of the first tick of time, where the dream of form began. But what seems like many years in dreams is merely an instant in reality. The illusion and fantasy the first thought of humankind projected was that they were separate from the one-mind of Creation, a reality we've never really left at all.

Shockingly this dream state of mind projected an image of itself to block out the real world. The human body was perceived as what seemed to be an animal-type body that had thoughts separate from the *One Thought of Life* that they came here from. They were decidedly separate from their Source—God—and no longer whole, it seemed, and they were different and separate from each other.

Time became what seemed too distant from God and their urge to pull away was constant, giving them disturbing and insecure sensations. On the level of the body, we humans are similar to animals. All the basic bodily functions, pleasure, pain, breathing, eating, drinking, defecating, sleeping, the sexual urge to find a mate, and of course, the sensation of birth and death we do share with animals.

Man's history book began compiling pages as we humans became constantly obsessed with insecure thinking—and these thoughts fragmented more and more thought with the concern:

"We are more than an animal." This became the truth for the first humans to walk the planet, the image they made staring them in the face. This was too disturbing a truth to tolerate.

In the symbolic first relationship, Adam and Eve saw an image of nudity and scarcity, which made them afraid. Thoughts of denial with their nature set in quickly. But they were also afraid to go back within to the reality—the wholeness they projected themselves out of. Their guilt for doing so kept them even more separated from reality and continues today. Rather than being willing to tap into the knowledge of what was truly real, their unwillingness piled on more guilt and shame. As the guilt evolved so did the image of the human body, and living with the threat of the unknown matured with it.

Their history portrays plenty of indecisiveness and panic that repeats itself in the world today. As thoughts fragmented into bundles of more thought, the same as the splitting of cells, the word "time" was validated, and it had a frightening and worrisome tone in its definition or lack thereof.

As projections continued, humans were everywhere and were haunted by this separated thought system they continued to defend. Now committed to separation from their Source, more and more insecurity and unawareness of what to do next or what to expect, with the discovery of certain body parts and bodily functions increased their unsettledness. Their sexuality was so confusing they labeled it taboo.

As new fears flowed in, existing fears compounded. The light of their reality was obscured and not bright enough to be friendly with their animal nature, to allow it to *be* and yet enjoy that aspect of themselves let alone to go deeply into it, and find Divine guidance hidden there. Humankind was lost.

* * *

With history mounting errors, it became difficult to find reality within this dreaming state of mind. So humans did whatever was necessary for survival, and their newly formed ability to make judgment helped make decisions of "right" and "wrong." With the discovery of time, science was born and they accepted this dream as their reality.

The more they questioned their own thoughts, the more their uncertainties began forming images of one another that changed with time and with right and wrong attitudes being formed. The more they saw themselves as having a body, the more they questioned this possibility. Their uncertainty of the body raised more questions about their origin.

It wasn't long before religions began arising and disassociation became pronounced as the "you are not your body" belief. Countless people in the East and West throughout the ages tried to find their creator, or some form of enlightenment to save them from this uncertainty of who and what they were. Many began to deny the body of certain pleasures and of sexuality in particular, where fasting and ascetic practices began being explored. They even inflicted pain on the body trying to awaken or punish it, because they regarded it as sinful.

In Christianity some practices were considered mortification of the flesh. Others tried to escape the body by entering trance-like states, or seeking out-of-body experiences. Many still do. Even the Buddha is said to have practiced body denial through fasting and extreme forms of asceticism for six years. But he did not attain enlightenment until after he'd given up the practice.

The fact is no one has ever become enlightened through denying or fighting the body, or through out-of-body experiences. Such an experience can be fascinating and can give you glimpses of the state of freedom from material form, but in the end you will always return to find your body is where essentially transformation takes place.

Let's understand that transformation is through the body, not away from it. Why, when all along I've been suggesting the body is illusion? It's because had we *not* separated from our Source and projected the image of the body, we would have no need for transformation. But remember, we never really did separate from God, we only dream we have. Thereby, the idea of transformation is using the body, or using the dream of having a body, to go beyond it and rise above it to our true light. In other words, to awaken.

Later in this book you will discover why the body is the means to get you there, the doorway through the "fence," if you will. This is why no true Master of Spirituality has ever advocated fighting or leaving the body.

* * *

If we consider the ancient teachings concerning the body, only certain fragments have been preserved, such as Jesus's statement that "your whole body will be filled with light." Other fragments have only served as myths, such as the belief that Jesus's body never turned to dust, but rather ascended into Heaven. Where did his body go? Almost no one to this day wishes to explain or try to understand these fragments or the hidden meaning of such particular myths. Why are they hidden? The ego always hides from the truth.

The belief that "you are not your body" has prevailed universally, leading to body denial and attempts to escape from the body. Countless spiritual seekers have prevented themselves, because of this, from attaining spiritual realization for themselves and becoming finders.

Is it really necessary that we continually try to recover or question the lost teachings on the significance of the body? This is where more fragmenting thoughts pile on with existing fragments. This becomes the birth of further separation. I've discovered there's no reason for all that.

All true spiritual teachings originate from the same Source. In that sense there is only one Master, who manifests in many different forms as a reflection of His Light while we dream of separation, or live in this world. You are that Master and so am I, when we access the Source within. The way is using the body to go beyond form. We must go beyond the dream to that Light watching over us while we sleep. We do this by noticing Truth, which is the Light.

The Light is where your real relationships take place and then reflect in this world as a manifestation of this reality. Your real relationships reflect from your inner awareness of the light Jesus spoke of; otherwise, they project from unreal thoughts of fantasy wishing. You are going to learn to know the difference so you can make right-minded decisions.

Even though all spiritual teachings do originate from this Light regardless of the laws or doctrine scribed by man once they become verbalized, they are no more than a collection of words, more form. But you can choose to consider them as directional signs pointing you back to where you belong.

The first humans were so overtaken by guilt and fear they didn't realize that leaving the garden paradise was unnecessary. They separated by choice. God didn't order them or drive them out of Eden, but their newly formed separated thought system made by the ego-based mind did. They were afraid to return to the garden and to let go of separate ways. They no longer understood the light of One-mindedness, *and that confusion lingers today.*

* * *

What you perceive as a dense physical structure called your body, subject to disease, old age, and death, is not ultimately real and certainly is not your totality. It is nothing more than a projection that gives a misperception of the nature of your *being*. Your true *being* is the Oneness of the light that connects you to your Source. But don't turn away from or deny the body, because behind that projection is concealed the splendor of your eternal essence. This is your true reality.

Don't turn your attention elsewhere or attack yourself with untruths, as within yourself is where your search for truth will be complete. It is one step through the door of the fence. It's the step you must take in order to know your eternal essence, or, *being*. As you step you will feel pulled through the door like a magnetic force and your relationships with the reality in others will strengthen and flourish. It's a brotherhood you share, so don't fight against your body or your brother's/sister's body, because in doing so you are attacking your own reality.

You are your body only as you project its image. The body

that you see and touch is only on a thin illusory opaque screen, portraying what you believe yourself to be. Behind the screen is your true reality that is the invisible you—life manifested. The real world.

"Consider music," I've learned from Dr. Wayne W. Dyer. "Isn't it the space between the notes that manifest the song?"

Each of us is the song of the *Manifested One Life* that is birthless, deathless, and eternally *now* with no past or future, says Eckhart Tolle in his book *The Power of Now.*

Why, then, have we all been sharing the same problem of not seeing our relationships as part of the Oneness instead of simply *being it*, as it I, and sharing only *that*!

Could it be possible our focus is too concerned with the body itself, instead of what exists through the fence? Or, is it that we have the stage fright to revert back within as it was back at the Garden of Eden only an instant ago as we dream?

Meanwhile, histories everywhere play out in different schemes of time and space and form, always looking to a future that cannot exist. Why?

All that we ever have is reality, which is that crystal-clear instant, *now,* where past and future mean nothing. It's a *holy instant*, and it carries on endlessly. It's that infinite non-dreaming unseparated thought where we're all in touch and whole with our Source, which I've chosen to call God.

Chapter 7

Projecting Conflict

It should be easy to understand that when we get angry conflict is born and leads to attack. Even the thoughts of condemnation types of judgment are attacks. Thoughts are either real or unreal. Here's why:

A thought will either project an image or it will extend by reflection of the light of truth. Everything in this world is either true or false and of love or fear, with no in between. That said, nothing is partly real, almost true, or slightly unreal.

Our Source of life is only love, and only joyful and peaceful experiences result. Only real thoughts of love—which is truth, unity, and wholeness—can extend. A projected image does not extend because it is imagined thought. The thought perceives an image. An extension cord extends the electricity, but it surely doesn't project it. Do you project love, or do you extend it? Your loveless thoughts project images of attack and can be seen as a portrayal of your life if this is the thought system you choose. The way anger plays to our fears may not be so easily accepted.

Anger and fear are always involved in the projection of the self-made thoughts that are separate from your Source. Consider being at a movie theater. Have you ever had the image on the projection screen extend itself into your lap? Hardly. The image is projected and there it remains until you turn on the light, lift the screen, or turn off the projector. The clarity of the image depends on the brightness of the light in the room. The image may seem real, but it doesn't last. The image has no real source, because

31

somewhere it ends. Sooner or later it perishes.

The thought of God is His Love or Truth, which is one and the same and extends lovingly and truthfully with no end or no limit. Think about it, have you ever known a conceivable limit on the truth? Have you ever known love to be unreal?

The images we do project are our responsibility, not God's, because we made them outside His Thought. When we blame others we only fragment through projection more separated thoughts, making for an unreal, confusing show of images. We get angry from images of being attacked. But we see our own attack on someone as justified, and believe we're in no way responsible for it. Actually, we feel it is our right or an entitlement when blame supports it.

With these sorts of beliefs we conclude that the other individual is equally ready for attack rather than love. What else can be expected from this insane unreal picture other than strategies for conflict, or even war?

Why do I say it's an unreal picture? After all, I see it with my eyes and have emotional responses to what I see. What is real is of God and extends forever. A projection has no traceable real Source. The image can only be traced back to its projector, which is manmade and of a separate thought—that cannot be whole, because of its separate status. We can say the Garden of Eden's "bitten apple" is the symbolic beginning of separated thought which formed images. The tree of knowledge projected a thought of the unknown: *"Hmmm, how curious, a tree that has knowledge. Shall I taste its fruit to see what flavor I may find?"*

* * *

From one individual to another, which one of them is thinking real? Are they thinking from a reflection of their true light or do thoughts arrive from a projection—dreaming types of thought? If our trueness and reality is not reflecting onto the dreaming mind, then the conflict between the two is the insanity of thought separate from God. The thoughts lack wholeness.

The only way to bring sanity out of this insane thought system made from separation, produced by humankind, is to accept that your true essence, or, your light, cannot conflict. After all, how can total oneness conflict? This is what proves, at your innermost core, that you are responsible for what you believe. If we are of the One Mind of God, and our thoughts illuminate from this light, would your beliefs be real or unreal? You wouldn't need curiosity to find reality. You are already it and are your pure knowledge.

As you continue through this book try to keep in mind that when a situation has been given wholly to the truth, conflict cannot arise. In other words, if two individuals are both operating from the reflection of this *One-Light*, which is *Truth*, how can an attackful situation arise? This must mean that peace is all there can be.

In this peaceful joining where you meet with real thought, it is a wholeness of mind opening to its knowledge, instead of a segment of mind wishing it were separate and dreaming so. From *joining* comes the state of mind where you begin to perceive situations as meaningful. Truth is the goal and is where real opportunity will come your way. You will begin meeting the right people at the right times. Astonishing proof of this is revealed in my book, *And I Knew My True Abundance*.

If you have not yet, then I encourage you to check it out when the time is right for you. You'll see why nothing outside of wholeness or total oneness of mind can mean anything substantial to your life.

* * *

Nothing in and of itself can attack or become attacked. But images can seem to attack, and that is why bodies seem to attack other bodies. Remember, even a thought of attack is attack in your mind, because an image is projected. You may not see yourself as vulnerable to your separated, dreaming thoughts, but when you see attack as real thought, it is only because you believe the image you project of yourself is capable of being attacked. You've learned this from those who taught you this is an unsafe world.

Let's be patient now while we go into some deeper water for just a moment. But don't think too hard about this, just like you wouldn't panic and struggle to make brisk strokes in a calm but deep end of the swimming pool. Rather, let yourself smoothly swim with ease. Simply absorb what I have to say, here, and allow it to become a part of you. Okay, are you ready?

When time began it made you see attack as real; it's ticking away at life, the serpent conniving Eve, and even the image of God's angry outcast on the first couple from paradise. You have the effects of these self-made thoughts being projected as images and they are embedded in you, which are also the effects on you that control the way you live your life. If you can comprehend this law it will ultimately save you, but you could be misusing it. You must begin to learn how it can be used for your own best interests, instead of against them.

Look at it this way: Consider when you project attackful types of thought are you not fearing attack as well? In that sense, if you fear being attacked this must be proof enough that you are certainly vulnerable. This gives you vulnerable and defensive attack thoughts in your mind, which, of course, are frightening thoughts. If it's a frightening thought it must be projected and somewhat confusing, whether you care to accept it or not.

The fact is, in order for us to be completely invulnerable to attack, we simply cannot have a single attack thought. Doesn't this make sense? It would then make further sense, or let's say, an "extended" sense, that invulnerability and attack contradict each other and will not compliment any given situation.

Any idea you have about attack stems from the thought that you always attack yourself first. If you believe you can have attack thoughts and at the same time be invulnerable from attack, then you are attempting to weaken yourself in your own eyes. How and why is this? The answer lies in the fact that you are in conflict between being invulnerable and wishing to attack, and conflict only weakens us. You have also attacked the perception you have of yourself. Additionally, because you believe in these attack thoughts, you can no longer believe in yourself.

A false image of yourself will always struggle to take the

place of what you truly are. When you struggle, conflict is all through you. Operating in this fashion makes it extremely difficult to handle any irate situation you may encounter. But, hey, it could just as well mean the difference in that slippery, sliding putt on the golf course as in my story earlier. Was it my task to sink the putt or was it more important that I didn't have any conflict in that task? Think about the task, surely, but don't make a struggle out of it.

As the late great golf instructor Harvey Penick says in his *Little Red Book*, "When I ask you to take an aspirin, please don't take the whole bottle." Taking conscious steps toward the true outcome you want is more whole than a reckless advance.

Too many of us distrust anything unfamiliar, whether it's a sliding putt in a fun game like golf or a conflict-free loving and joyous relationship. Turn the page now, you've survived the deep water, and let's move on to discuss by example how all of this plays out in the *special love relationship*.

Chapter 8

The Same Old Play of Thoughts

Here's a fun story I've told before early on in my book series about conscious steps for understanding a love/hate relationship. You know, that wonderful feeling we have toward each other in the beginning, but then in due time we get caught up in confused feelings over why we're in the relationship, except this time I share it in a different way to help us shift out of our darkened ego-based thought and into the light the Holy Spirit provides us.

Eve just returned home from a long day and thought she'd relax for a while as she waits for Adam's return from the jungle. As he walks in the door he goes straight for the sofa, tired, but content. Adam has much he wants to tell her this evening. As he removes his shoes he yawns and stretches his arms back behind his head, then kicks up his feet onto the coffee table. Adam is talking about his day as Eve continues to head into the kitchen for some wine.

She brings two glasses and the wine bottle to Adam for him to open. She knows he likes to open the cork and savor its aroma. He's wearing the shirt she picked out for him as a special gift a few weeks ago. In fact, she loves the mischievous air it lends him. He takes life so seriously. Eve loves these times, when he's relaxed and lets himself go in conversation.

Adam is trying to relieve the stress his tree-cutting business often places on him. Being tired of course helps. He rambles on about a situation at the job site today where twelve trees severely needed trimming, but only eleven of the twelve trees on that property did his company trim. It seems the owner of the land insisted that the big old apple tree in the center of the property remain untouched.

Eve doesn't find the subject particularly interesting, but at least he's talking and opening up to her. He's relating and she notices his stress level reducing. She gives him another moment.

While he talks, she advances toward the sofa, feeling lustful and sensual. She has a spontaneous urge to kiss him right there and interrupts his verbiage, just to celebrate the moment. For once, she decides to initiate foreplay instead of him all the time, a responsibility he complains about bitterly. Now is her chance to surprise him.

Adam is watching her from the corner of his eye and smiles, while taking the glasses of wine and setting them on the table. He responds to her first kiss with visible pleasure. But the more she insists to go further, the worse it gets. She definitely senses that he's uneasy. She feels his entire body stiffening, as if refusing any further involvement. He's still smiling, but his face is frozen. He has stopped talking and reaches for his wine.

Adam is visibly uneasy, and Eve can't figure it out. But she thinks maybe she can, and tries to, because she doesn't like the vibes she's getting. The truth is that when she initiates foreplay, it never goes very far. It seems it's never the right time, and he may even say he has a headache. Eve would think part of him is still a little boy afraid of his mother, and he wants nothing to do with her. But, oh, how she'd love to send her little darling back to her all wrapped up and labeled "damaged goods."

* * *

On the other side of things if we look at this picture from how Adam is projecting it, we see it a little bit lop-sided.

Eve had already been home before Adam, and as he walks in the door her scent is in the air blending with the warmth the late afternoon sun sends through the open windows accompanied by a gentle autumn breeze. She looks lovely with her hair tied back. She asks him in a sensual tone if he'd like some wine, and of course he accepts. He loves it when she's in this type of mood and caters to his every need and whim. At times like these, life is beautiful. Adam feels lucky to be pampered in so many special ways. He feels special.

While Eve goes to the kitchen, Adam talks about everything and anything just to make her laugh, because he knows she likes the chatter. As he's talking, he suddenly feels the urge to make love to her. But, ahh, … if she'd only make the first move, which she hardly ever does, then he'd heat right up to her. But what luck, there she is offering herself to him in a kinky way, and fantasy has now become reality. But something is wrong. Is her intensity way too exaggerated? Such forward behavior feels cheap and upsets him. It's as if her life depended on it, as if any man could satisfy her now.

She has set her glass on the table and cuddles up, kissing him. Now she is begging him to say, "I love you." He thinks maybe he should make a recording of those words so she can listen to it all day long. The situation is beginning to get on his nerves. Is it sex she wants or love? Where does the need for affection come from? He is confused. It's a need so great, it seems that he dare not get too close for fear of being controlled like a puppy dog. He quickly passes a thought, a thought he's had before. "Didn't she have a father?"

After about the seventh kiss, Adam stretches out an arm to get his glass of wine. He hopes his uneasiness has gone unnoticed, but knowing her intuition he can never be certain. Spilling his wine on the rug is a thought he thinks might be a solution, but on second thought Adam decides to go to the bathroom to compose him and stall for some time hoping for a new attitude.

Now, by this time, Eve is thinking he is running away again, but this time she won't run after him. She's had enough of this male indifference. Enough of acting like a nice girl. Enough of making his favorite meals and fulfilling his bedroom fantasies, in exchange for the affection never given. Eve's anger begins to mount and she decides to give him the silent treatment. What she wants to say seems too awful, too vicious. Five minutes ago she wanted to kiss him, but now she wants to get even. If only he'd come out of the bathroom.

* * *

Now let's take a look at Adam's thought process as he stalls for time in the bathroom. He reproaches himself for an attitude. "After all, she did all of that just to please me." If he'd follow her initiative for once … If he'd give her the love she expects, it would end the petty war of the past few days. So he returns to the living room full of good intentions.

He finds her distant, cold, snappy, and all curled up at the end of the sofa. He's now thinking of her as a "Jekyll and Hyde." His good intentions have just been dissolved. He quickly thinks to himself, "If it's war she wants, then that's what she'll get." He won't be manipulated like this! Besides, ever since she's been visiting that *snake* of a therapist and begun to assert her, it seems the problems have only increased. Nothing gets by her.

Then she starts one of her tirades on commitment and his blood curdles. He swallows a gulp of wine to calm down, but it tastes like vinegar. In a flash he seems to have grasped the heart of the problem. She's nothing but an inconsiderate, jealous little brat! Everything she touches she tries to dominate. Another ruined evening, and he's only one thought in mind, which is to leave.

He tries to interrupt to tell her, but she takes the words right out of his mouth. "I suppose you want to leave again," she blurts. "Perhaps you think I'm disturbed? Or that I am disturbing to you?" She continues, "Besides, do you honestly think other women are any different? After all, *we're all sisters*, isn't that what you once told me? Did you think I forgot?" Now she goes for the jugular, "Do you really think another woman would put up with your crap? Look at yourself, you're pathetic!"

* * *

What I've just described is the *special love relationship*, which we will be discussing much as we move along. This is how it seems to go, on and on, again and again. The song of blame and accusations. The tune will escalate. Doors will slam. Somebody will leave and return. A revolving door. There will be a few screams, a few tears, bitterness on both sides, contrition, a little kiss, a peck, and on a good night there will be makeup sex. In a few days, or a week or so, it will begin all over again. Sound familiar?

I know, you're probably thinking that this only happens in your living room. Sorry to disappoint you, but it happens everywhere around the world. Of course, you will add your own touch just as I have done before.

In some areas around the world there is physical attack, even murder, to go along with the verbal abuse. But in general the scenario doesn't vary that much. Sometimes you'd think that human love relationships follow a predetermined program.

She says that she's ready for a man who is capable of commitment. Or, does this mean she has a *chain* she's anxious to use? She wants him to give her what her father never could. But the fear of such expectation is too much, particularly because he has no idea what intimacy is, either with others or himself. He understands power, fame, mechanics, and ideas. But emotions are something else. He lacks the main ingredient in this love recipe, the ingredient she claims to have herself. As a result, he feels worthless at the emotional level.

He feels guilty for not responding to her lifelong dream and knows he cannot adequately fit the expected role. She's unhappy for not being able to make him happy, no matter how much she tries to help him become the prince charming of her dreams. He feels controlled, manipulated, forced to be what he's not. He felt the same confusion around his mother, who always *wished* him to be a prince. It is a replay of the same old dream. She has the same grip on him without realizing it. She doesn't realize what a burden her dream is. He has no idea of the weight of his demands, nor his negligence. He's not aware of his behavior being the cost he makes her pay for her dream.

This is how he manipulates her, making her try so hard to reach him. This is how it slowly becomes unbearable. For her, it's as though she waits for him and follows him. And for him, who is silent, he runs away. All their actions betray what they hope to obtain from each other, and both are deceived.

Each of them, individually, keeps up the same game, anyway, be it maliciously, to see how far the other will go before giving up the dream. They go on out of hopelessness, and when they do finally have enough of the maneuvers, when they have sufficiently trampled each other, and have used up their entire arsenal, they will break up in disgust.

She will say she has once more been taken for a ride and was abused. He will say he's once again fallen into the same trap. Both will suffer because it didn't work out. For centuries, partners in the *special love relationship* have danced to this same old broken record.

Chapter 9

God's Mind Is Set on You. It Doesn't Change.

In order to know the wholeness in another, you must first know yourself as being whole. You have a willingness to know this for yourself, otherwise you wouldn't be reading this book. So let's begin by me suggesting that you try and see if you can put yourself in touch with the following statement that *A Course in Miracles* gives us through its endless lessons. This will help you to see that what is beyond yourself will either make you fearful or loving. There is no in between, and only love can be whole.

> *Time and eternity are both in your mind, and will conflict until you perceive time*
> *Solely as a means to regain eternity.*

To regain something surely indicates that you may have misplaced it or lost it. There is nothing about you, or beyond you, that can be taken away. This is important for you to accept and is so because *you* are all there is to reality. *You* are eternity itself. This puts you beyond time. I'm sure you're thinking what a confusing thought this actually is. But you won't be able to totally grasp this notion as long as you believe that the attack thoughts, as well as the judgment thoughts you have of others, are caused by factors outside yourself. Since nothing is outside of you, there can be no factors there.

If you can understand that God is not magical or mystical, and that His Creation is simply the Oneness that He is— and you are of *that*—then you can begin to realize you and I or another as being of this Oneness, too. It is the One Mind of God.

Everything you contemplate that is of love which is Truth circulates this One Mind where we are held as God's one Idea— His Creation. But for now, forget about me and let's discuss you for a while, until you grasp this notion of oneness, and then we'll move toward discussing *us* as the wholeness of the real world.

Nothing but you exists in the reality of One-mindedness, which is your Totality—or God. Yes, that's right; the total of what you are is God. Therefore, how can you, who must be reality itself, attack, have attack thoughts, have conflict of any kind, or be attacked, when God created only you? If you have been looking on yourself as a body being all that you are, then you are having a tough time answering that question. The "you" that is beyond your body is infinite, and since infinity cannot have a sum of separate parts, you are Creation in Its totality. But so is the reality behind my own bodily form which is of this same Oneness—or wholeness.

What you and I share in this wholeness is a brotherhood with our Father being the Totality of Creation Himself.

We can use the word brother/sister to indicate this inner connectedness within the One Mind of Who we are—God. But let's not get all hung up on a word. For centuries we've been allowing words to have a dictated meaning, something seemingly set in stone to label an idea and identify us. Rather, let's concern ourselves with the meaning behind the word.

In your imagination as you live humankind's dream of time and space and identities, is where you cannot fully understand eternity. It is this understanding that governs time, which is the dream. This is where you seem to be able to violate God's Laws. But in the real world God has no such laws because total oneness has no use for them. Without the illusions that you project as the earth, and bodies, and yourself, that you think you see around you, those entities would not exist. Remember, if the projector is removed (your separated mind) images are not projected. So what remains?

* * *

What is it that can cause you to be upset or to get angered except for something temporary, like a projection? Likewise, how can anything temporary be real if God's Creation is eternal? You are this creation, but as long as you dream of separation your mind carries with it a permanent aspect the Holy Spirit. He is in you—the essence behind the dream.

Being that the Holy Spirit *is you*, your eternal reality is established. He is your Guide while in the dream state and is using time for your gentle reawakening. Thereby, the Holy Spirit is eternally you and temporarily in your right mind, while you dream of separate thoughts from that of creation, keeping you responsive to your One-minded eternal and whole existence. However, your dreaming perception may view things as opposite or upside down to the Oneness you truly are. In other words, your perception may side with the dream as being true reality. Try to look at it this way:

We all have a wrong-minded or upside-down state of mind about us that insists we're seeing the truth on particular matters, and we even go out on a limb to prove to ourselves and to others our so-called righteousness. But this is okay. Now we can face up to this and learn that we each have a right-minded sensation or *gut feeling* if you will, that sees through our wrong-mindedness, whether we care to admit it or not. It's that sense about you that may not always be precise, but is on a precision path to the only truth, regardless of any brave front we may portray just so that we might gain instead of lose. It's this "something" in us that gently whispers the true thought that there is no need to have to prove ourselves.

You can choose to either live your life in fear, which only places the defensive untrue statement in your mindset, such as "I'm not afraid of anything," or you can choose to be honest with yourself. If you're not fearful of the ultimate, then fear itself would never enter your mind. Every response you make to all that you perceive is either up to you, or illusive thinking. The latter, or ego, is the wrong-minded approach to making its own truth, because it cannot comprehend total Oneness, which is what rests beyond everything that is called Truth.

The ego only understands what is of the body. This wrong-minded part of the split-mind has fragmented from Oneness of thought as it dreams. This is why it cannot realize being at-one with anything, especially itself. On the other hand, the right-mind is what holds on to the sensation of a one-minded reality. In the right-mind is where the Holy Spirit abides so it can whisper real thoughts while He watches over the entire dream. He leads you to certainty about yourself and to the fact that you are with Him as the Spirit of God.

God doesn't change His Mind about you, because He isn't uncertain about Himself. Therefore, the next time you are uncertain about anything which you feel might be life sustaining, or bitterly important, ask yourself a quick question. Why am I uncertain? Next, listen for the answer.

* * *

God's knowledge is available to you as well as *It* is to me, by the Holy Spirit's method of communication through the right-mind. But be aware that the right-mind, too, is separated thought, just as wrong-mindedness is, but only with a positive perception wanting to follow the truth, and with a willingness to not look back.

Just remember the Holy Spirit is the *unseparated* thought system we share that is of Truth. It's that non-dreaming wholeheartedness in each of us that keeps ourselves—the dreamer—alert to the reality behind the illusion of form. Whereas the wrong-mind is the illusive thoughts and perceptions that keep on insisting you are separate from God, and that His Divinity, Heaven, is outside of you.

This "insisting" is ego based and upholds itself as right when it always puts emphasis on saving itself. It fears death, whereas our right-mindedness can perceive the essence beyond the body.

This is the perception that you are more than a body, and we can call this *right-minded perception*. It is this perception that bridges you to One-mindedness.

But let's not confuse the wrong-mindedness portrayal of dishonesty and disparity as that of you who dreams. Rather, wrong-minded thoughts and perceptions are totally of the dream itself, or ego-based mind. This is your ego that has no sense at all of Divinity.

The ego is so fragmented in its thought that oneness can never be brought to it. It is impossible. What is unreal can never join what is real. This is why the ego in each of us can never accept total truth. How do we help the ego that is in all of us to see the light? We don't but, rather, we let go of it by leaving it be. Like all thought in dreams, it fades away, until a point where the dreamer totally awakens.

God created you in eternity as Himself, not a body as the ego-based dreaming mind would interpret reality. God gave us the power to create so that we are like Him. This is why your mind is holy and is not of or inside the body. But as we discussed earlier on, let's not get all caught up in the word *holy* as meaning something special, or outside yourself, or appointed, that requires special clothing, water, oils, or beads, etc., but more so, see the word in your mind as a signpost joining your brother/sister on the right-mindedness bridge that leads us Home. Allow your own *holiness* to prove your Divinity.

Try to accept your Divinity as simply being or knowing your true essence that leads you to your true free will in life. It's what you truly are and not what you pretend to be out of fear. There is nothing beyond Truth, because your free will is one with His Will. Once you begin tapping into this knowledge by getting accustomed to its quiet messages from your Communicator, you will realize how much is up to you, which is everything.

When anything threatens your mind like attack types of thought, simply ask yourself one quick question. Has God changed His Mind about you? Then move on by accepting that His Mind is changeless, and refuse to change your mind about yourself. How could God ever decide against you without deciding against

Himself? Besides, when you live a life of wholeness, what decisions could there possibly be that does not reflect truth? It's the same truth that is your brother's/sister's.

Chapter 10

The Illumination We All Share

A Course in Miracles suggests through many messages that we're often too busy thinking we have many different problems, but we really have one—and that is our separation from God.

Consider people when they are in their thirties, they worry about losing their looks. In their fifties, they worry about losing their capacities, and a little less concerned about their looks. By their seventies, people worry about losing everything: control, relationships, and their very lives. As times of our lives pass on by, we lose our hair, muscle power, memory, strength, and agility. We lose our taste buds, libido, and the ability to have a good night's sleep. We're always worried about something coming along to interrupt our life. Losing *something* is always a fear.

Hippocrates was the first to compare life to seasons, and aging to winter moving in. Long ago Horace wrote about time in that, "Sad age comes. Farewell to laughing, happy love and easy sleep." Chateaubriand called time an "ultimate shipwreck." On his sixty-ninth birthday, Whitman called himself "an old, dismasted, gray and battered ship, disabled, done." In 1936 Freud wrote a letter to a colleague about time giving him the chance to "look forward with longing to the journey into the void."

Mary Sarton in her sixties enlightened me where she wrote optimistically that the joys, peaceful times, and the relationships of her life have had nothing to do with time and an ultimate end in this world. She said, "They don't change. The morning and evening light and flowers, music, poetry, silence, the gold finches darting about ..."

Time only exists in your lifetime here in this world, and as it does people sometimes stop being able to buy their own groceries, or go to church without help from a loved one. Marathon runners' legs fail them. Golfers' backs, hips, and knees go out on them. Bikers give their bikes to their grandchildren. Champion athletes worry about making it to the bathroom. People begin feeling about their bodies, as Yeats put it, that they are "tied to a dying animal."

With any given number of words, it's easy to explain how the ego operates and what it is all about that points to a realization not easy to explain, but can simply be better realized with one word. Truth.

When a thought arrives *to* the brain it's either of a self-projected image or it's a thought that has no projection, but is a reflection of the light of truth that certainly extends. What do I mean, here?

Let's be honest and ask ourselves where does Truth come from? Did we invent it? Or, did we project it and if so, what does its image look like, or can we rather agree that Truth simply has always been what it is? We can then say its extension has been extending forever without a starting point. Nothing needs to be constructed in order to extend. An extended thought is never partially extending, but always consistent and is what Mary Sarton was able to see in the meaning behind light.

Each of the two thought systems is extremely opposite: God, or the ego-based mind; unseparated extending Truth or its opposite consisting of hunches and partial loyalty to both at the same time is impossible. For instance, how can what is true sometimes be partially true? On the other hand, illusion is always illusion, and regardless of any kind of constructing will forever remain unreal, and never has the potential for becoming true. This is where Freud looked at time as the journey into the void.

But everything that is unreal, such as time, does have a truthful thought tied to it which is the fact of its falsity. The Holy Spirit uses illusion as well as truth to show us that the results of each are as different as their foundations—rock or sand—and we can't really vacillate between them while being one with our Source.

* * *

We all choose, whether we realize it or not, one of two roads in life. The old and the young, the rich and the poor, men and women alike will decide their destiny and how they live in this world.

One is the broad well-traveled road of mediocrity; the other is to greatness and meaning. The range of possibilities that exist within each of these chosen destinations is as wide as the diversity of the gifts and personalities in the relationships we choose. But the contrast between the two destinations is as night is to day.

What I mean is the path to mediocrity places limits on your potential. The path to greatness in all that you do including your relationships unchains and realizes your potential. The path to mediocrity is the quick-fix short-cut approach to life. The path to greatness is a process of sequential growth from within. It is a mission in life.

Travelers on the lower path to mediocrity live under the laws of the ego-based mind, which include indulgence, scarcity, comparison, and competitiveness. Travelers on the upper path to greatness rise above wrong-mindedness and all its influences and merely choose to become the creative force of their lives. One word expresses the pathway to greatness. Choice. Those on this path have dug out their *choice* and inspire others to find theirs.

Let's carefully consider why *A Course in Miracles* teaches us that "Nothing alive is fatherless, for life is creation," and the *Course* continues this lesson by asking us to contemplate this question: "Who is my father?" and, further asks, "Would be faithful to the father we choose?"

Depending on how you choose to answer, you may have a conflict of interest. If you choose to see the ego as your thought system and surely you did make the ego, then how could the ego-mind have fathered you?

This choice gives you an authority problem that is your source of conflict, because you made this separated thought system with the use of your wishes, for how you'd like the world to be, you think. But you're not certain.

No true free will, only fantasy wishes, is the state of mind where you must either make the ego your father, or its entire thought system made from separate and different wholes will lose its legs to stand on. Or, we can say it will lose its footing in its sand-based foundation.

* * *

The unseparated real Thought of God creates by its eternal extension, while the separated dreaming part, or tiny segment, of the mind projects its images to coincide with its wishes. The *unseparated* is whole and has no separate parts that need standing on. It doesn't wish, but merely knows what its own wholeness is creating. There's no second guessing. Try to consider it like this:

Think of God's thought as light, and you are a ray of this extending illumination. Since the source of this light is of infinite abundance, the rays forever illuminate. The closer you get to the center of this thought system, the clearer and brighter the light becomes. On the other hand, the more you get caught up in the web of the ego's tangled thought system which weaves a veil obscuring the light, the more unsettled and indecisive the dark shadows seem to be due to lack of light. The lack becomes less and less a lack and even the slightest spark or little flicker is enough to shed some light into your dreaming state of mind.

By holding the light to the darkness you can see your way to a potential starting point to living your true free will. Yes, some of us may just need enough light to approach the starting point, where others will need encouragement to continue their already taken steps to freedom. Take an honest look at the way you've been traveling thus far.

The one and only Truth will support you as solid as rock and give you confidence for the journey. Truth is the Oneness that you comfortably and securely are and does not pull you in different directions, which illusion is so capable of. Did you make up the many reasons for the many directions of illusion that presents you with the confusion over reality? Did you make yourself, or were you created by an extension of Thought Whose Idea has come—a ray of light.

When you are willing to see your inner reality with Divine Light as being of God, then so will the world around you see themselves the same, because we are a part of each other. We will come to know the ego's foundation as too fragmented, and fragile, and cracked apart for the required support necessary, to not only have a successful life here on earth, but with the relationships that support our purpose and match this success. Even when we slip from time to time through the cracks and seem lost, it will be okay, because the light will shine into the tiniest of crevices you'd ever imagine.

Leo Tolstoy has written, "Each time of life has its own kind of love." Begin seeing that the Lamp of your *unseparated* mind is always lit—and *that* illumination is what you and I are. It is our true reality and pulls us through the cracks with each other's help. We can say that God *leaves the porch light on.*

Chapter 11

The Image of Your Guilt

It's our own choice when we condemn ourselves and judge others in this same manner, which brings on the guilt that spurs attack-type thoughts. The mind chooses to judge another as being unworthy of his or her love, and believes punishment should be due. Often it is as tedious, but hurtful, as the "silent treatment" used in my story a few chapters ago taking place in the living room of the young couple, Adam and Eve.

The mind that judges perceives itself as separate from the other and believes that by punishing the other it will escape punishment or some other kind of loss for itself. This is an untrue attempt of your mind to deny itself reality and to escape the seeming penalty of denial. What is the penalty? you ask. It's not in the laboring sacrificial tasks of getting rid of denial that penalizes you, but it is in your holding on to it. By holding on to it your guilt obscures the extension of your Father's Light to you.

Try to consider it this way: If you have a lack of truth you continue to harbor this insane, unreal projection of guilt which is a dark existence. Its image is your body and nothing more. The piling on of guilt for hiding this truth from yourself is the penalty you pay and it keeps you focused on the unreal. What you have is illusion giving you more illusion until the bitter end of your relationships, career, or anything else you pursue in this world, including what you call *your life.*

When we accepted guilt into our minds collectively it has been seen as an illusory form of wholeness being so fragmented that it started the multidimensional world of separation, another illusion. But just as well our acceptance of the Atonement, the process of reawakening is what heals the guilt we feel so that we can make the proper right-minded choices in our lives here on earth.

The completion of this process called full *Atonement* ends this world. This is at the last and final tick of time, with no more images projected, where wholeness will be forever reestablished over illusion and fantasy with awakened oneness. Time will no longer be needed. This will be the final undoing or reversal of separated thought. Just take a look around you in this world, watching the television news, reading the newspaper, and consider what it is you really see. Our eyes are glued to it as if we want more of it. It is an addiction, and we always do receive more of it because we make it so.

You will note a world projecting punishment, leading us deeper into fear. We're always apprehensive and afraid of the consequences of any action we take, good or bad. If punishment or loss or disaster happens to someone else, we feel safer in that ours was not due. The laws that govern this image seem to be the same laws that dig our grave sites.

Newborn babies arrive into the world in shock and a smack on the rear sends them screaming at their first breath of air, from a process we see associated with pain. How often has a baby arrived gurgling joyfully and peacefully, with a cute smile? They grow up to be taught to beware and to guard against what surrounds them, and quickly learn to see the sadness and death that they ultimately expect for themselves. Their mind becomes imprisoned in the brain and bound there. The mind will be formed by the images that are governed by the laws of the body. The mind seems to marinate inside the brain like an olive in a martini. The mind becomes even more controlled by the intoxication of illusion, especially if the body is harmed, or threatened. When a body is lost prematurely to death, not one of these youngsters has had time to soak up the image of a cruel God, but their adults have.

While this is not what a father wants to subject his children to, we see this as the price to pay for love. But why must we see love as requiring pain, agony, hard work, or sacrifice as a way of strengthening it? There is no cost for love in the real world. If it did cost a hefty price, according to the ego's interpretation, attacking others would be justified and seen as a way to gain peace and joy. Isn't this why we've been going to war?

Only the world of guilt could enforce this, because only guilt can conceive of it. Think about it. Back at the symbolic Garden of Eden, the separation portrayed as the loving first couple's so-called sin would not have projected outward what we are seeing today, had they not believed it was their Father who drove them out of paradise, as punishment.

* * *

Imagine before the separation occurred millions of years ago, but only an instant ago in reality, that nothing existed except for perfect oneness where it was free of guilt. There were no cares, no worries, no anxieties, only continual bliss with perfect calmness and quietness of mind. Sounds like Heaven, doesn't it? It certainly is, and this is what time is meant to accomplish for us.

The purpose of time is to get us back to this state of *Being*, which is what we already are and always have been behind the dream of separate guilt complexes. The bliss of Heaven is our reality—our natural state of mind. But because of fragmented reasoning we continue to dream of the path to mediocrity, which is littleness. Being away from our natural state of greatness where we truly belong merely increases the guilt with time. But time also can heal the guilt, fear, and separation.

This is why God placed the Holy Spirit into our dreaming segment of the mind, which places Him as the right-mind, so that He can participate in the dream. He is constantly through reflection, teaching us how to awaken carefully with the same calmness and quietness we naturally know so well. Once this goal has been accomplished, we will no longer need our Teacher, or time in which to learn. We will have awakened as the Teacher, with lessons completed and wholeness existing.

* * *

Although time is being used by the Holy Spirit, our beliefs seem to be that the time it does take humanity to awaken leads us into the future. This is not accurate.

You see, the Holy Spirit is not governed by time and uses it in His own way. Time is His friend in teaching, and not a single instant is wasted as it ordinarily seems to be by the human body. Each instant of physical time has its purposes in the arranging of events, as orchestrated by Him who conducts from each of our right-minds. Yes, He has used time for that gray hair, or *no* hair, those wrinkles that you may sport in that distinguished age compared to your rebellious long-hair teens, which also served a purpose. This is the real universe in performance.

So what can you begin doing now? Send reflections of your trueness into your projected images of how you see the world. Begin being who you are and not what the world expects of you. Actually, the world doesn't expect anything of you, but you think it does.

You must realize that the Holy Spirit *is* your right-mind, and time is in your brain—the body which is a character, a figure, in the dream of form. Time runs your character of the dream but not the character of your reflection that is eternal.

Time moves along with your body and when your body passes on and ends, so will time. This world is projected; the images you make will not go with your body, because both will have ceased being a dream of what could never become real. Even your brother's/sister's projections will no longer exist without you in this world. How is this? you ask.

You see, without the projected images you make of others, these individuals don't have an image to live out. The world stops without you in it. Projections end. Their images projected by their own separated thought play off of your images of them. Without you, form doesn't exist. Your fragmented thought is what made the world you see.

This is why all your wasted time is due to your identification with the ego, your body, which uses time to make destruction on

56

the world. The ego-mind, just like the Holy Spirit, uses time to convince you of the inevitable end to learning.

However, to the ego the goal is your death but not for itself, so it thinks. The ego-based mind tries to figure out a way to live beyond the grave, even if it's hell. Its failure to prove this is its frustration and its fear. But on the other side of things, the Holy Spirit's goal is your vision of the eternal instant of life that you live inside of. He teaches us that this is as certain as God, and that this certainty is your essence which always exists, *now.* Understanding the present instant, *now,* leads you to accepting and realizing your own holiness.

The holiness you truly live as your reality is not the image of your guilt. Therefore, what else could it be?

Chapter 12

Holiness Releasing Guilt

Do you often choose to live as a victim? There is a belief much of the world has that they are helpless. In her book, *Living in the Light*, Shakti Gawain has written about "victim consciousness," where basically we think the world, people, and economy, and more do things to us and that we have no choice but to accept the standard set by outside powers.

As the oldest of six children rose in a lower-income but loving family, where both parents worked full-time jobs to give their children the best life possible, I believe that is what set the stage for my determination to be the best I could be. I was always one of the smallest boys in school, and my father used sports to drive me above my littleness. To both our elation, I excelled.

Magnitude certainly took over where my own "victim consciousness," or, littleness, thought it lived. But I was also taught, as were my parents by their parents, and soon, that whatever happens to you as a child shapes your character and personality and governs your entire life. Likewise, the limits and parameters of your life are set and basically you can't do much about it. We grow into adulthood with this mindset.

In the year 2007 when I turned fifty, I was imprisoned into the Ohio prison system with inmate badge number 542280. I experienced things that were so repugnant and grotesque to our normal decency that I shudder to repeat the details ever to anyone. When family and friends have often asked me to describe prison, I simply tell them it is an ugly beast and a true hell, plus some. It is what it is.

One day near the beginning of my incarceration where I lived in a tiny cell for several months, clothed in rags and limited to a shower but twice per week, I became aware of my real freedom. A lesson indeed would somehow be brought forward in my mind.

I discovered a freedom that was beyond what the prison guards, ranking officers, and other staff, along with a full line of intimidation tactics and oppressive belittling and ridicule could take away from me. They could control my entire environment, they could do whatever they wanted to do in abusing me, but I learned quickly that I was a self-aware being who was able to look on as an observer to my very involvement. Within due time my real and basic identity was intact. I could decide within myself how all of this was going to affect me. I felt a victim of uncalled-for abusive behavior, but began to change the channel of thoughts that were sinking in.

* * *

Later, but in due time, in the midst of my experiences not only with prison personnel and guards, I would learn to extend my thoughts to a different picture, one of writing about what I was learning. Or, I'd prefer to look at it as rather than learning, what it was that was coming forward in my mind. As I began gradually to put my thoughts onto paper I could see a book one day being published with all that I had to share. As the author I'd see myself involved with speaking and lecturing to groups about this newly found consciousness. The victim had faded away.

As time moved on for me behind bars, one thing led to another as they always do and I was seeing a clear picture, but with something missing. It was a feeling of needing to touch something spiritually, but I didn't know what it was. There was a missing piece to the puzzle, my puzzling thoughts and perceptions about what I'd been puzzled about all my life? This is the time when *A Course in Miracles* found me in prison. I get tears in my eyes and a dry throat every time I think back to when my eyes set sight on that old musty copy of this publication. It was that little flicker of light that magnified and illuminated my path ahead, and it is why you now hold this book in your hands.

Through a series of disciplines—mental, emotional, and moral—while enduring life for the time being behind bars, I began to change my mind. The world was taking on a different look, one that no longer controlled me.

I principally began using my memory and imagination until it grew larger and larger to where I had more freedom than my captors—state government employees, "state babies" is what they'd call themselves—who left their own prison each day to go home to another atmosphere. They had more physical liberty, more options to choose from in their own environment, but I had more internal power to exercise the options I did have. I'll use the description "accessing the power-source within" only to lead you to its title, which is *holiness*.

* * *

As I slightly indicated earlier but in a different way, the word *holy* when we think of it has taken on a religiously dogmatic meaning over centuries of misuse. It appears as though it is something owned by a power outside and higher than us. Somewhere along the way the ego-based mind has placed a tag on it as "out of reach," where we must get on our knees and bow to it and beg for salvation but I'm sorry to disappoint your ego, *holiness* is not above you nor is it a power outside of you. It is your own power at its truest state, and at a level that is in your comfort zone.

Think of your own holiness as fuel. What good is it to identify your fascinations and goals if you're out of touch with yourself, no comfort zone, or too stressed out to pursue them? Being in touch with the holiness about you—I mean taking care of it so you can always access it—is your power.

Consider the finest performers who befriend their *holiness* as one might another person. Look at Olympic athletes who demonstrate such grace under pressure. They are in touch with their inner holiness. Successful relationships know how to share this holiness among one another even under the toughest of times. We can say, relationships, too, must perform under pressure.

The renowned Harvey Penick offered this advice to his students who became golf champions: "Be you. Do as you usually do … It is your mind that will have the most to do with how you play the big match. You want to stay in the present."

We all have and share this certainty of holiness, and we must come to realize its truth. It is in all of us at all ages and the different stages in our lives while we're here on earth.

Our holiness is certain because it is of God. It can only be shared because it is what created God's only Son. The wholeness we share is His begotten Son, and it is not limited to one individual. This holiness I speak of is the one ingredient that delivers wholeness to our hearts (mind). As a human, Jesus was well aware of this and this is why he is our leader in the process of the Atonement. He acts as our model for eternal life as our elder brother in the Sonship. The reawakening process is important for us to understand, because this is where we communicate with each other from beyond physical form identities.

* * *

Holiness is the air about us or the essence that's of our true knowledge that cannot be taught, but we can become aware of the potential that has been hidden. It's an awareness that can be acquired.

When you display this trueness and real life joy to others it catches on and is your blessing to the world. They will want what you have, which leads them to acquiring it for themselves in their own due time. We give blessing to others when our natural joy is extended, which is an example of real, unseparated thought, rather than a projected image where no one can decipher its realness.

To bless is another word that has been misused and misleading as some sort of magical sprinkling of Divine Security. But once again, don't get caught up on the word or let it stop you from being yourself. Feel free to accept its meaning as it reflects in you, because it is the meanings you give away to those you encounter, not a word, which performs a true blessing. When you give me your blessing, which is love, I feel better, which is to heal. Make sense?

You can see the reality behind illusion is healing the split-mind, because you are acknowledging One-mindedness, and this is holiness. It is a blessing because the thought releases you from guilt no matter how temporary it may seem to be. You've accepted the knowledge that's always been within you, only hidden by the guilt you're releasing.

In all of this you have not counted yourself as being unworthy of holiness, because your natural knowledge supports it. Holiness is yours without the efforts and sacrifice of formal training or special ceremonies or rituals, and these are fine if this is what *truly* makes you happy. But since it is not of the brain, *nobody* can be trained to be holy.

Chapter 13

Don't Deny Your Knowledge

While in prison I began writing the comprehensive notes for this particular section of this book. Waiting for my approved early release was a source of my own tension. I was standing on top of my footlocker a foot off the concrete floor using my top bunk as a desktop. Overcrowding had double-bunk conditions in the tightest of places.

It was at the double bunk next to me a close thirty inches away and another bunk on down the line where neighbors in this open bay dormitory were in a heated argument with tempers escalating. I was seeing all hell break loose. Physical violence is an everyday event in prison. No one would win this conflict only to result in both participants spending thirty days in the hole, unless the situation could come to calm. A segregation cell is neither a pleasant nor a healthy experience. I spoke up firmly to interject, which is not my normal practice, because minding one's own business is highly regarded as an unwritten law among inmates.

Angered myself, I harshly blurted out in a serious tone, "Gentlemen! Please try to understand that we're all miserable in here in our own way!" That was it. Nothing more was said, and the conflict cooled itself with no guards involved or such repercussions as a "hole shot."

The world is filled with denial and without mere direction it seems that some type of proof of the truth is usually needed before we can open our hearts to it. We've all at times played the "doubting Thomas" role due to the pressures of denial. Let's even go further to say it's our decision to refuse knowledge. If this is the case, it seems the world has a logic of its own that leads to nothing and to a goal of illusion.

If we decide to have all that we can and to give what we can, and still continue to be nothing but living out a fantasy, then we're only projecting our thoughts into oblivion where unreal thoughts are stored. This keeps us living among images in the awakened state of mind and sinks us deeper into the dream of a separate universe. Let's not think, here, of a physical universe such as the stars, planets, moon, meteors, and galaxies, but by all means do enjoy its glorious reflection of our reality. Let's think more so, of the real universe, which is nonmaterial. It is the One-minded true thought system that is the Idea of Creation itself. You and I are thought, and this Oneness is the real Universe that is our Divinity, and no nuclear holocaust or cosmic convulsion can ever wipe it out.

* * *

Let's begin seeing that the physical universe you see with your body's eyes is a projection from your separated mind, but with hints of reflection from your reality helping to supply the dreaming thoughts. Does this make sense? I hope so, because if you're seeing a universe that is splendorous and glorious and filled with awe, then you are reflecting Divine holiness into the separated segment of mind that only thinks it is separate.

On the other hand, if you see a universe full of fear, destruction, loneliness, emptiness, and darkness, then this is a projection of your guilt that is blocking your reflection of the light you are. What you are is an integral part of the Sonship—the sum of all of creation.

In this sense of reflection I've just described, there can never truly be an end to the world. But you will eventually open your eyes and awaken where all projection has ended, where what you've been reflecting all along lives on. Likewise, if you think you have and are and give everything, but you're not accepting this because you lack proof, then you are denying a thought system which you are closing off, and you have wholly separated from the truth. How do you wholly separate? By denying and avoiding the truth you know is within you.

Consider how often we've heard it lectured to us by a parent, grandparent, or other close relative that is much your senior, that "when we die we will have been lucky to have had at least one true friend" and we buy into this. Consider additionally, that this is why God placed His Holy Spirit in the part of your mind where you placed separation, form, time, and space.

* * *

When we see with the body's eyes we're projecting outward, but when it's in a reflective state the whole mind is telling the brain what to project. This is where right-mindedness prevails. If our thoughts are totally wrong-minded our thought system is of darkness.

Our thoughts are mixed, a combination of right-minded and wrong-minded thoughts and perceptions by your choice. We're constantly either projecting images or extending truth through reflections as God's whole child, but we do so as either the dreamer slowly awakening or as a dream character. Remember, only a tiny portion of the whole mind thinks it is dreaming.

In other words, the thoughts we share with God are beyond the beliefs of our projections set by the world, which you think you are part of. We make our own beliefs that are not of our creation. It is these beliefs as a dream character, rather than Truth, that we choose to defend and also *try* to love. Then there's the occasional thought: "How dare someone try to take these beliefs away from me!"

But you can choose to turn all of your beliefs over to the Source of your knowledge, which you've been denying yourself of, from within. The Holy Spirit will undo whatever is necessary after He sorts through the truths and untruths you've been living under, making sense for you so you're aware of what it is you need to know. There is nothing in the world that can teach you that the logic of the world leads to nothing. The crowd you are following may not be aware of their own nothingness, but the Source of your inner holiness knows everything.

Any direction you take where the Holy Spirit has not led you goes nowhere. Anything you deny that He knows to be true, He must teach you not to deny it any longer. He must begin your lessons by showing you what it is you absolutely can never learn on your own.

Start by asking yourself, are you beginning to see a clearer picture of why you made the errors that have haunted you? You see, the Holy Spirit is inducing the simple truths into your present self-made, world-taught, thought system which has become so twisted, tangled, and split and fragmented and twisted more, being so complex of an illusion that you cannot see it means nothing by falsity and fantasy. As the truth is accepted, an undoing of this complexity occurs.

The Holy Spirit will simply survey your self-made foundation, the house you built on it, and if necessary take a wrecking ball to it, level it, clean away the debris, and rebuild it better than you can imagine. All of your errors that built this nothingness have already been forgiven. Who has forgiven you?

The Holy Spirit has, which is you. This is why you're able to overlook all the fantasy you once believed and see beyond it to the wholeheartedness you know reflects your true self. Not only is this forgiveness of yourself, but you've opened yourself to the knowledge within you.

But first, here's what you must do:

You must accept the fact painlessly and guiltlessly that you cannot, alone, reverse or undo these errors in thought. You have chosen to deceive yourself long enough, and are what built the ego-based mind. Begin, now, in this very instant, to understand with calmness and without worry, that the deception and ego are both unreal, and trust that you are not alone.

But how can you begin to trust when all along everything seems to fail you? Ask yourself one question and then seriously listen and contemplate the truthful answer you receive: If God has no ego, then how can you?

Chapter 14

Exercise: My Holiness Is Deep within Me

We all have our bad days, moments, and periods of dire frustration. If it's not one thing, it's more of something else trying to get under our skin. This exercise has helped me achieve extremely beneficial results when finding me lost, alone, and away from my reality. I have written this meditation using various principles contained in *A Course in Miracles*, as well as from insight of Henry David Thoreau in his various essays where he expressed ideas that helped him through times of loneliness and despair.

This is designed to help you realize that your unique holiness reverses all the laws of the world. We'll go beyond all the laws of time, space, distance, and limits of any kind. The holiness that you are is totally unlimited in its power because it establishes you as an integral part of the Sonship—at-one with the Mind of God.

Through your own holiness the power of God makes manifest. His power works through you. In other words, the real you, your true essence, is necessary in the creative power that is available to each of us. There is nothing this power can't do. Your own holiness can remove all pain, can end all sorrow, and can solve all problems. It can do so with you or in connection with anyone else.

Look at it this way: If you are holy, then so is everything God created. But the most important part of this for you to grasp is to see this in a different aspect, which is, all that God created is holy, because you are. Is this an arrogant thought to have? Only to the ego.

Try to see in this sense of wholeness, that you are all that God created and nothing else. Without you there is nothing else because there would not be a Whole Son of God. The wholeness of God cannot exist without you. This is why you must thereby be eternal. Isn't this simple to understand when you look at it in this light? Once you can accept this as pure knowledge within yourself, your individual holiness will illuminate everywhere in a confidence true to your heart.

Now that you understand this part, the idea of the exercise ahead will eventually bring you to overcome completely the sense of loneliness and abandonment that your separated thought system can often experience. Depression is an inevitable consequence of separation. Likewise, are anxiety, worry, and deep sense of hopelessness, misery, suffering, and intense fear of loss. All of these and more are reasons for the many problems plaguing relationships. Think about it. Can you really extend love when you are under the gun of these bad guys?

* * *

The separated thought system of this world has invented many "cures" for what is believed to be the "ills of the world." One thing these cures don't do is question the reality of the problem. Yet its effects cannot be cured because the problem is not real. The idea in this exercise has the power to end all of this foolishness forever in your mind. It may not seem like foolishness to you while you're experiencing them, but it is terribly so foolish, despite the serious and tragic forms it may take.

Take some time now while you absorb my message and try to think as deeply as you can, but do so naturally, within yourself, that everything is perfect and radiates through you and in the minds of all the world. This is *not* foolishness. The radiance illuminating from you will heal all sorrow and pain and fear and loss, because it will heal the mind that thought these things were real. Keep in mind that this mind you are healing has already *suffered out* all of its allegiance to these harmful thoughts.

You can never be deprived of your perfect holiness, because

its Source goes with you wherever you go. You can never suffer because the Source of all *healing and joy* goes with you wherever you go. You can never be alone because the Source of all life goes with you wherever you go. You may say you already know this, but you continue to seek for Divinity outside yourself; your prayers, etc. ...

It's quite understandable that you do not believe all of this, because the ego-based mind has made your beliefs. How could you possibly understand this when truth is deep within you under a heavy cloud of insane thoughts, dense and obscuring, yet representing all that you see? But now you must make your first real attempt to get past this dark and thick cloud cover, and simply step through it to the Light beyond.

* * *

Choose a period of time each day that suits you best. Sit quietly for three to five minutes with your eyes closed. At the beginning of the practice period repeat slowly to yourself: "In this situation involving my (*hostility*), there is nothing my own holiness cannot do, because God goes with me wherever I go."

Be sure to substitute a word or phrase that fits your situation and the problem you suffer from, whatever that might be. The illusive feelings of your separated thought system that are bothersome to you must be addressed. Try to get a sense of turning inward, going past all the idle and wasteful thoughts of the illusive outer world. Try to enter deep into your mind but with minimal effort, relax, keeping it clear of thoughts that might divert your attention.

Please note the "minimal effort," because straining and tightening you with squinting eyes is nothing more than trying to exhort brain energy. This is not what this or any of our exercises, prayers, and meditations are about. The key is to relax, and the amount of time should be brief, because it is bringing forward the holiness in you that is important here.

From time to time throughout your day you may want to repeat the idea as reinforcement. You're trying to sink down and inward, away from the world and all its foolish thoughts. You want to reach past all these things. You want to leave appearances, by approaching your reality. This is where you clearly reach God.

In fact, it's extremely easy because it is the most natural thing in the world. It's called "being your true self." You might even want to accept that it is the *only* natural thing in the world. As you naturally go deep within yourself, with your eyes closed, you may experience a mix of colors racing across the darkness of your shut eyelids. I have often experienced a glow of white luminous light around particular images in my mind. For me this has become routine.

The way will open up to you if you know, instead of believe, that it is possible to be in touch with your innermost self. The exercise can bring startling results even the first time it is attempted, and sooner or later it is always successful. As this book opens up for you, we will be going into more detail about this kind of mindset that will advance you along your intended path. Isn't it really about love?

Use this exercise and tailor it to your comfort zone, and find a time of day where you can make this a routine, so you can banish all the problems that are holding you down, or making you feel like a prisoner. Believe me, I do know that being a prisoner is no fun. Let's repeat slowly with eyes closed: "In this situation involving my (*loneliness*), there is nothing my own holiness cannot do, because God goes with me wherever I go."

Think effortlessly about what you are saying; what the words mean to you. Concentrate on the holiness they imply about you. Contemplate the everlasting companionship that is yours, and on the complete security that surrounds you. You will begin in an instant to laugh at your thoughts of turmoil by remembering that *God goes with you wherever you go.*

Now you're ready to explore why we *wish* for that *special relationship*, and the fear involved, which is the fire that seems to burn us.

Part II

You and the Special Relationship

Chapter 15

In This Instant Is Your Reality

Take a quiet moment, now, an instant in your mind's eye, seeing yourself going to a funeral of a loved one. In this instant you're driving to the funeral parlor or church, parking your car, and getting out as you glare up at broken beams of light trying to break through a cloudy sky.

As you walk inside you notice flowers arranged beautifully with soft organ music. In that same instant you notice faces of friends and family as you find your way through the room. You feel the shared sorrow of losing, the joy of having known this individual that radiates from the hearts of those present. You reflect a unified purpose for being there with others. The person in line next to you turns and gives you a nice smile.

As you walk to the front of the room and look inside the casket, you suddenly come face to face with *your* body. This is your funeral, a few years into the future. All these people have come to honor your life, to express feelings of love and appreciation for your contribution to their life.

As you take a seat and wait for the services to begin, you look at the program in your hand. There are to be four guest speakers.

The first is from your family, immediate and also extended; children, and others who have come from all over the country to attend. The second speaker is one of your friends, someone who can give a reflection of your character and your devoted friendship. The third guest is from your work or profession. And fourth is from your church or some community organization

73

where you were involved with service.

What character would you like them to have seen in you? What contributions, what accomplishments would you want them to remember? Look carefully at the people around you, what difference would you like to have made in their lives? How have you touched them? All in this same thought as you slip into the next instant, you are honestly and truthfully receiving the answers.

One of the answers has arrived; you've touched in these instants of thought and have glimpsed, ever so briefly, your deep, fundamental, and natural values. You've established brief contact with that inner guidance system at the core of your true essence; you've found your own holiness, the center of your light. You have discovered and communicated with your spirit, the Holy Spirit. You were briefly in a no-time zone called a *holy instant*, and sooner than later a false idea of which you are, the ego, has crept back in to convince you that time is your reality.

* * *

The ego is not a friend of time, but uses it in order to gain its way around the world. It doesn't trust life and fears death, because it doesn't know what to expect with either. The ego-based mind's strange religion must teach you as it convinces itself that there is a future beyond the grave. It tells you that by not following certain rules your future will consist of burning in hell for eternity. This is its primary scare tactic. It speaks to you about Heaven, but insists, you're not ready without further and particular preparation, always at a cost or sacrifice.

But, consider, if the ego-based mind tries to teach you these types of lessons, then who teaches the ego? That's simple. You do. This is why the separated thought system the ego lives by is such a vicious circle of illusion.

When you identify with the ego you can't seem to escape the belief in hell. The guilt and fears keep you there. The ego preaches that hell is always possible no matter how prepared you are for Heaven. Not a single individual that follows the ego's guidance is without fear of loss, and especially death. Yet ask yourself:

If death were thought of as an end to pain, would you still fear death? What a strange and seemingly contradictory question that may nonetheless have a true answer.

The ego must try to keep fear from you and then bring it back to you again, so that it may maintain your allegiance. It wishes to keep you on the roller-coaster ride of up and down illusions—the fantasy of thrill while impressing fear upon you. The ego-based mind continues to convince you that Heaven has not a guaranteed spot for you, and it pushes this on you right up to the time of your body's final breath.

* * *

Hell is the most frightening aspect of the dream of separation, and fear of hell is why our guilt for separating from God's Mind is so heavy. It's a dream of guilt, where the *figures it represents* carry the burden.

But in truth the Holy Spirit teaches and assures us there is no hell and Heaven has never declared you an outcast. You've never left, nor will you ever. We can say that Heaven is the fluffy white cloud you fell asleep on that comfortably holds you in place while you dream. Your reawakening is carefully progressing.

The belief in hell is what prevents you from understanding the present, only due to the incessant time restraints your ego has on you. You're afraid to understand anything as timeless. The Holy Spirit knows only the present and uses time to undo fear, where the ego makes the present useless. The ego needs the past and future in order to look back and blame while seeking ahead for further fantasy, all for its survival. There is no escape from fear in the ego's use of time. It will use time as a device to continue piling on guilt making a mountain of vengeance.

The Holy Spirit has the constant task of undoing or reversing all of this in the present moment. Fear is never a result of the present and can only be made from the past or in predicting the future, which neither truly exist. Each immediate instant, now, stands free and clear from the past, and certainly has not touched the future. What is *now* is always *now* and is never past or future.

A moment from *now* becomes a fresh untarnished, clean new instant. In this reflective state the present extends forever and is our glimpse of eternity. The "now" I speak of is your immortality.

Take this thought just a bit deeper and ask yourself, what truly is time without a past or future? It has taken *time* to misguide all of us so completely, but it takes *no time* at all to be what you are, *now.*

Begin your time in this instant, now, to practice the Holy Spirit's use of time as a teaching aid to happiness and peace. Start in this instant to see that this is all there is of time. After that instant, feel yourself naturally and suddenly with no effort entering another instant and proceed from there. You will find that nothing from the past can reach you here, because in this instant, now, is your existence. This is called the *holy instant,* where your own holiness has no fears.

We cannot conceive of time without change, yet holiness doesn't change. Ask yourself, in this instant, now, does hell truly exist in your mind? How can it? Heaven never changes within you, because it is who you are always, and *always* is in this instant. In my book *Mastering Your Own Spiritual Freedom,* you will discover that "You" are the Kingdom of Heaven. *A Course in Miracles* says to us, "It is in *you* where there is no change in Heaven."

This must be so, because there is no change in God. In this holy instant in which you see yourself as free from the past and no threat of the future, is where you will remember God. I say "Where" you will remember God, rather than "When" because the holy instant is not a period of time, but it is the place "Where" your mind exists—and your mind is you.

* * *

Let's look further beyond to see that remembering God before we separated into a dreaming state of mind, is the aspect of ourselves that lives in the absolute truth.

Just think about that for an instant. Truth. Isn't this the light in how we know ourselves regardless of outside influences? That said, who and what am I without the past or fears about the future? Then ask again, how long is an instant? What is it that measures this instant, now? Give this instant to the Holy Spirit, and He will give you glimpses of eternity. Have the goal of being inside a holy instant as often as you can.

When you give this holy instant to Him, you are also giving it to your brother/sister, because the Holy Spirit is in each of us. This instant is never yours alone because it's always shared. When you are tempted to attack another individual, you are operating from outside your holiness, which can only be of the ego-based mind.

The holy instant is the same length of time for your brother/sister as it is for you—if you wish to compare eternity to time. Practice entering a holy instant by making a simple statement to the Holy Spirit—which is yourself, and say, "I give this instant to you so you may undo or reverse or correct the anger I feel." This is a sure way to leave behind your anxiousness, unsettledness, despair, depression, or any number of unreal thoughts haunting you that are not of your real self. Then, be done with it; wipe your hands clean and move on to the next instant of your holy and true reality.

ext, it's important that you realize you've entered a new, clean instant on behalf of the entire Sonship—the totality of all creation beyond form, by losing the past to it and keeping the future from it. All of your success in this world comes to you within the holy instant, including your relationships that you'll soon discover are holy, too. It's your reflection instead of a projection you see in them.

his vision through holiness is real and is your escape from guilt and your acceptance of what you are, which is one with your Creator. So how long is a holy instant?

It can only be the time it takes to realize the illusion of your anger is not what you truly want to experience. Is anger an error in thought as well as all your other miseries that only keep you limited? Certainly. These are the thoughts that are not of love that come across a separated mind.

The holy instant takes you into your immortality and to your creations. I hear you asking in this instant, what are my creations?

Anything real as a result of you. How about joy and its effects? That which is a real creation of yourself can mean exchanging your thoughts of an illusory hell for true Heaven. Or, your willingness to transcend the entire ego-based mind's making of fantasy, and "ascend" yourself into Heaven. After all, Heaven is within you.

All along this is what Jesus has been trying to teach us when he once said, "Do this in remembrance of me," putting the ego aside and appealing for help in miracles from your brothers/ sisters everywhere, by living within true reality—wholeness of mind. *A Course in Miracles* suggests that we "offer the miracle of the holy instant through the Holy Spirit and leave His giving it to you, up to Him."

Chapter 16

The Reality behind a Relationship

The cup or chalice in medieval legend used by Jesus at the Last Supper, and subsequently the material object of many chivalrous quests, has been a subject of a prolonged conscientious effort to uncover its whereabouts. Its history has been everywhere. In the novel by Dan Brown, *The DaVinci Code* suggests many clues to the undiscovered Grail hidden in the works of artist Leonardo DaVinci.

In the days when the newly formed church outlawed speaking of or writing about the much-shunned Mary Magdalene, her story and importance had to be passed on through discrete channels, such as the arts that supported metaphor and symbolism. A perfect example is the portrayal of the Last Supper. We can quietly gaze at Mary Magdalene's long red hair and quiet eyes where we see something in the expression of this beautiful woman that echoes loss of a loved one, but not a loss of love itself. Is the chalice merely a metaphor for something far more important? A message for humanity?

Perhaps down through the centuries and more so in recent decades, many have had suggesting thoughts of a romantic relationship between Jesus and Mary Magdalene, and that she indeed was a spiritual woman, and was not the prostitute image the church had wished that we project. If they were a loving couple, then so is it as a blessing.

But this is not my point, here. My challenge to you is, could it be that our own mirroring of each other is where we will discover the real Grail, which we have not been very willing to accept? Could this unwillingness to overlook the ego be why we've not yet uncovered it? It is the oneness of mind we must discover in ourselves and by accepting this instead of a separated ego-based thought system, our seeking is over.

The Holy Grail in and of itself is really not the cup that held the wine Jesus drank from, literally. It's in the cup's content as the bloodline Jesus was holding. However, unlike Dan Brown's novel by Anchor Books, which led me to my conclusion from the physical, it is the Divine Blood Line called *Christ* that all of humankind shares. Here is the Holy Grail discovered, after all. But please bear with me here.

At the Last Supper, Jesus shared that message not only with the male apostles, but as well with his female loved one, life companion, or, wife, if you'd like, Mary Magdalene, seated at his right side in communion together as *Christ*. Jesus wanted us to realize Christ and receive Him in the feminine, too, as well as the masculine.

For reasons of fear, not love, our ego-based thought system all along has chosen to think in separate terms of man and woman, rather than the one Son of God, regardless of sexual gender in the dream of duality. Time has been and continues to step in to heal this misinformed projection made by an erroneous thought process, separated from true reality.

* * *

For centuries within the dream of separate identities, talented individuals everywhere have been inspired to express all of this, by extending their own reflective thoughts in a fashion that may accelerate healing through their discrete messages.

We can look at some of the most enduring art, literature, and music that esoterically try to communicate history, such as Mary Magdalene and her actual, real relationship with Jesus. In addition to DaVinci's messages there were Botticelli, Poussin, Bernini, Mozart, and Victor Hugo that all whisper of the quest to restore the banished sacred "feminine," and bring her in line with the masculine. Legends like Sir Gawain and the Green Knight, King Arthur, and Sleeping Beauty have given us symbolic illustration.

Before his bodily form exited the dream of life, Walt Disney's hidden messages dealt with religion, pagan myth, and stories of the subservient goddess. It's in Disney's tales like *Cinderella*, *Sleeping Beauty*, and *Snow White*, all of which dealt with the sacred feminine. Nor did one need a background in symbolism to understand that Snow White, a princess who fell from grace after partaking of a poisoned apple, was clearly an indirect mention of the fall to temptation of Eve in the Garden of Eden.

The Little Mermaid is a spell-binding tapestry of spiritual symbols so specifically goddess related that they could not be a coincidence. *The Little Mermaid* actually portrays Ariel's underwater home as none other than seventeenth-century artist Georges de la Tour's *The Penitent Magdalene*, a famous special homage to the banished Mary Magdalene, the fitting décor considering the movie turned out to be a ninety-minute collage of blatant symbolic reference to the lost sanctity of Isis, Eve, Pisces the fish goddess, and reportedly, Mary Magdalene.

The Little Mermaid's name, Ariel, possessed powerful ties to the sacred feminine and, in the Book of Isaiah was synonymous with the "Holy City besieged." Of course, the Little Mermaid's flowing red hair was certainly no coincidence either. But the ego-based mind will make its way to provide us with its interpretation.

The Holy Spirit gives you the eternal *holy instant* to recognize things you'd not otherwise own up to. The function of the *holy instant* is to remove judgment entirely, because it's your projection of what has occurred in the past. Our past experiences are the basis for which we judge any given situation, as well as other individuals and the world we live in. But ask yourself, who made the past, your ego-based mind or God?

If we live in the past which is unreal, then how can we judge anything real? Judgment was not created, it has been constructed from a projected thought made by an uncertain ego-based mind, and seen by the body's eyes. Without the past, the ego is lost.

But we think we want the past and are afraid of not having judgment on our side, because we believe that without the ego our lives would be chaotic. We feel we *need* the separation where God is outside of us watching over from a place we *may* eventually go to. In this respect we are lacking in what we think is salvation.

In order that the ego-based mind may continually split and fragment its thoughts, like you'd see cells splitting under a microscope, it will need the past, which is how we learned of our false ideas and false needs. But we continue to think that *false* is *true*. Why does history repeat itself?

But we do often ask, "When will we learn from the mistakes of history?" and we do learn. But are we learning how to be better at judging? Or, is it we learn to closer define our individual needs that include judging? In this we seek out a more efficient direction for meeting these needs on our own separate terms. We think discovering a material object like the "Chalice," the finding of the Grail, will save us and set us free. Are you seeking magic or miracles?

* * *

If we accept the idea of the Sonship as *whole*, then we certainly can't pick and choose the parts we wish to love. This attempt to tear apart our natural wholeness is what projects guilt. It's this wishing of fantasy that plagues guilt in ourselves and carries over to our relationships, especially in those relationships where sex is involved and intimate feelings shared will guilt pile on when feelings are mixed.

During the act of sex, we are extremely close to this wholeness of mind, but upon its completion we run away from it. We judge and label what we like and dislike about our partner, and try to change what it is we dislike. We wish to make our partner perfect. This makes it difficult to realize truth in the relationship as a whole, keeping it unreal where real love remains hidden, "under the covers."

A Course in Miracles sheds light by teaching, "If you seek to separate out certain aspects of the Totality and look to them to meet imagined needs, you are attempting to use separation to save you. How, then, could guilt not enter?"

Our thoughts of being separate from our Source are nesting places for guilt, which are the grounds for lonely feelings. You see yourself in fear of your oneness with the individualized Self of the Sonship; Christ is the Son of God. This is what had transcended at the Last Supper, a lesson revealing everyone as the Christ Mind and not limited to a particular person, man or woman, yet beyond all form.

You may think it's too much to accept. It certainly is, as far as your ego is concerned. However, let's take a look at Jesus, our elder brother who leads the way in the Atonement process, where the Sonship is realized. Jesus entered the dream as a man who walked this earth and was able to reveal this oneness and extend himself beyond the dream of form and images being projected.

Jesus was not a magical man, but was totally aware of his wholeness. He sensed his wholeness as the Self of God, and he passed this along to others in a way they could understand at that time, where reflection was not as bright as it is today. After the crucifixion, the ego-based mind projected many fragmented and mounting interpretations. This is the mountain He meant by where Christ, not a human body, will arrive on top of showing humanity the path to the kingdom. The ego-based mind will have then been obliterated.

Christ is our reality, and is not lonely, especially when you can glimpse this sameness or likeness in others you come to know. But Jesus didn't deny this as we often do; instead, he accepted it and asked us to follow his same thoughts as a model. Think of what will transcend in this world when we all eventually are able to see and live by these modeled thoughts, not only in ourselves, but in our partner, too.

Remember, Jesus was able to be aware of both his true reality and the dream of separated thought. He had knowledge of projected images of guilt for the illusions they are. And then he truly lived in the *instant* of reality.

* * *

Likewise, the brushstroke of DaVinci's gentle touch on Mary

Magdalene's soulful eyes in the Last Supper is not separate from his Source. DaVinci reflects from the Christ Mind in himself the message that love is one and cannot be separate. If love and truth are one, we simply cannot love only parts of reality when reality is love and truth, one in the same. If we were to love opposite of Truth, which would be unlike to our Source, how can love be real?

To "separate away" is to make special. To the ego-mind being *special* has always been considered a good thing. We love our offspring; we love our parents because we are of them. But why do we think we love our special relationships? If it is separated out from our reality, opposite to truth, and we choose to see it as *special,* then how can it be real?

To believe that a special relationship can save you with special love is the belief that your separated thoughts are what save you. In believing this way, you are deciding that special aspects of the whole Sonship can give you more than others. The Sonship is one, the whole sum of creation less ego-based thought, therefore it is not special.

To believe it is special is your failure to accept this reality and is why you feel the way you do when you give yourself to another and later admit to yourself that "your guard was down." Maybe it was in a sexual encounter where you were wishing it would later lead and turn into something loving. Or, maybe some defensive play in questioning thoughts about your partner, like his or her ulterior motives, if any at all, has your feelings filled with doubt. Your past will convince you those "must be" ulterior motives.

Because of this mountain we've made of separated thoughts, all of our special relationships have notions of fear in them. This is why they are so back and forth in our feelings about the relationship being true. The *special love relationship* is not based on changeless love, and can't be forced to be so, which we often do. Any place there is fear, love cannot be depended on, because the fear keeps it from being perfect. Love can only be perfect and there is no other.

How many times have you heard it said and may have agreed with, that "There is no such thing as a perfect relationship?"

Thereby, because of these past lessons we accept that separated thought process as "wisdom through experience," and then proceed accordingly into a relationship with the prepared notion that we shall have to "work at it."

However, you will begin learning that the Holy Spirit has a function as the Interpreter of what you, along with your ego, have made. The Holy Spirit will use your special relationships which you have chosen, for whatever reason of support your ego needs, as learning experiences that will guide you as well as your partner to the truth about your role in the Sonship. This is why every relationship becomes a lesson in love.

Chapter 17

The Illusion of the Special Relationship

Let's be honest. I'd have to agree, wouldn't you, that we all want and need love? According to psychologists this is fact. Abraham Maslow placed the need for love directly above our needs for air, water, food, and shelter.

For many individuals, the search for love is frustrating and misdirected. Erich Fromm explained that "most people see the problem of love primarily as that of being loved rather than that of loving." Consider how we spend our time trying to make ourselves "lovable" with the right clothes, cosmetics, and conversation, then we wait for that perfect individual to come along and love us. When you really think about it, isn't this a sad way to live?

The frustration we fight comes from defining love as a product and not a process, waiting for fulfillment instead of actively extending ourselves. Love requires us to do something, such as reach out, act rather than wish, but to give of ourselves while speaking honestly of one another. In doing so we become active expressions of love. This expression is an extension of one's reflection; you, as the significant true essence that is the Holy Spirit, and He is aware of why you search for spiritual relationships.

Whether it's for romance, companionship, or even the fun golf-buddy-type relationships and so on, the Holy Spirit wants to help you see the light in them and not let you destroy them.

It is necessary that you do have special relationships, as

long as you keep in mind it is not where love exists. Whatever the unholy reason is in which you make a special relationship would possibly be, the Holy Spirit will translate it into holiness by removing as much fear as you will allow him.

When you place any relationship you encounter under His care, you are assuring yourself there will be no pain; however, you must be willing to have it serve no need but His. But it is ultimately for you.

Any guilt you feel in a relationship is from your ego-based mind's use in it, and the loving and honest and pure feeling of joy you have at times toward your partner is the Holy Spirit in each of you. By having this awareness you'll not be afraid to let go of your projected needs that will destroy the relationship eventually. Your true loving needs will not seem like they are needs at all, because love has no needs. It only requires that you be yourself and allow the Holy Spirit to take over from there.

Any relationship you make as a substitute for a lost one, such as attempting to make your past partner jealous by using another person, or any rebound attempt over the loss, the Holy Spirit cannot use. There's too much guilt obscuring the light of truth in you. But, not to worry, the Holy Spirit will begin ridding you of this guilt and it will make His task of doing so easier on your emotions, if you can be aware of this. But that's not always the case.

If you're finding yourself substituting, simply stop yourself immediately and ask the Holy Spirit for guidance and to quickly undo your errors in thought. Acknowledging to yourself what it is you are doing is a huge step in a direction for uncovering real love. When you see yourself as lacking love, you are judging your substituted relationship as having that same lack.

There are many reasons your ego comes up with in its use of relationships, and it is so fragmented that it constitutes you making more excuses and calling them reasons. Each fragmentation becomes a reality of its own liking, making you search for something that does not exist. Something that was never intended to transform simply will not transcend. In truth there is nothing it resembles, and therefore you seek for a reality you can't find, because the reality you think is possible is not real. The unreal can never be made real, but it can be substituted as being real by the ego-based mind. This is a huge trap many of us fall into.

* * *

There was a time in my early thirties when divorce was hitting me hard. The loneliness and sense of failure haunted me. The ugly legal proceedings and arguing over "who gets what" didn't help matters much. A few friends suggested, as friends will often do, that I get out more often, maybe got involved in the nightlife. My experiences in *that* are not going to be my point, here, but I'm sure you can imagine the negativity in that picture.

It was brought to my attention by another friend that a woman I'd been seriously involved with prior to my marital relationship had been seen on a given evening at an area nightclub. Our ending the romance was mutual and mostly due to Coleen's job relocation to New York as an artist. She received an offer she couldn't refuse.

The friend who informed me of Coleen's sighting has convinced me she was back in town to stay, and that I should try to locate her. I'd think to myself, "after all, our relationship was tight." So I did what many recently divorced men would do, I preceded on a mission to casually bump into my past girlfriend. I also wondered how things may have turned out differently had I joined her in the move to New York City. Then, my continued fantasy thinking told me I was now getting a second chance.

Being that this time period was prior to the technology boom of the 1990s, and that computer searches were unheard of unless one worked for the CIA, the FBI, or the IRS, my attempt of locating this lovely woman in the local telephone directory was unsuccessful. But I was dreaming of her blue eyes, long blonde hair, and that congenial smile which led me to draw up a plan in my mind that included hanging out at the particular nightclub she was spotted at.

Each weekend night for several weeks or so, I'd arrive at the bar in plenty of time to beat the crowd just to secure a seat near the end of the bar, and near its entrance. While sipping on my beer I'd imagine and wait for her to walk in the door with her elegant style surprised to see me.

I was prepared. My first topic of conversation would be focused on her artwork. I still had the colored pencil sketch portrait of famous golf professional Payne Stewart winning the US Open. She'd slaved over it for a good year, and it was now hanging in my office. I was so ready to get reacquainted, I thought, and in my perception of things the timing in my life couldn't have been better.

* * *

I'm sure you're realizing the illusion I'd been making of this and the disappointment I was setting myself up for. The fact is Coleen never did show up. In my own personal letdown, I would soon discover that she had indeed only on that one occasion made an appearance at this bar. It seems she was in town visiting her parents while she participated in a close friend's wedding. But, about one year later I did actually, and by accident, bump into her along with her new husband. Need I say more about the fantasy rides we send ourselves on?

The lessons we may have to take that teach us we're not our past does take time to sink in. The past is only a projection of altered illusion we try to make real. It is altered because the more time that goes by, the more we seem to wish to tweak it, in order to adjust the level of guilt we wish to project at the time of the past we're thinking about. There certainly is something to be said about saying "nothing like the good ole days." The past is *nothing* because you're always living *now.*

Living in the instant you're in *now* frees you from the bondage of old resentments or hurts. Or course, this does not mean you should completely forget about fond memories, but my point is your life and the relationships you have are much freer when you live in the *now.*

Think, too, about nations in this world if they were able to release centuries of conflict, prejudice, and suspicion that divide them.

The *Course* teaches us that "The Holy Spirit knows we build a frame of reference for the past, and He removes it for His frame of reference which is God. The Holy Spirit's timelessness lies here and in the *now*."

Chapter 18

You Are Limitlessness

Have you ever used one relationship by placing it at risk in order to gain another, or maybe to gain some sense of security? If so, how did you feel? If you've never experienced this, then how you do anticipate it would make you feel? Guilty, of course, can be your only true answer if you're honest in admitting to this occasional ritual many of us experience.

It would be over something extremely petty, but guilt is always guilt regardless of what level you may assign to it. It's always impossible to find something you don't like in a relationship and then find peace in it. The Holy Spirit teaches that all your relationships are seen as total commitments, yet not conflicting with one another in any fashion.

When you have perfect faith in yourself, each relationship you encounter will satisfy you without feelings of guilt. Why? Because you will feel secure with yourself in your own way of how you experience joy in each relationship that surrounds you. Your relationships will spring forward joy in each other, but guilt will sink in quickly if you try to make an individual into something he or she is not. This thought helps me remember a past relationship that began exciting with a nice woman, until certain rules she suggested I adhere to.

First let me say I have been an avid golfer all of my adult life and began learning this great game as a teenager. It's a sport I can take into my golden years. You could say golf is in my blood. It's certainly a passion that thrills me. I somehow developed a relationship through my business as a financial advisor where one thing led to another, and things were getting thick, and this partner in personal areas of my life at the time would ridicule my enthusiasm for this ancient and glorious sport. Demands were being set that I wasn't too fond of.

It was a fact her father had been an expert collector of antique trains all of his life since a young boy. He was proud of a marvelous collection that took up most of his finished basement. I certainly did find his collection an art and fascinating at that. My new girlfriend similar in age to my thirty-two years insisted that in order to expand our relationship I should cut back on my golfing "habit," as she termed it, and begin to take an interest in collecting trains.

She envisioned me alongside her father, attending the auctions as well as the train collectors' meetings, a subscription to a popular train magazine, and all that goes with being a full-fledged train collector, myself. This was to be my hobby in her mind. I must admit that my faith never did come forward in me about this becoming a successful, loving relationship. It came to a screeching halt, in its "tracks."

The reason we seek to change another individual is we lack faith in ourselves, and is due to our unwillingness to accept the fact that perfect love is within each of us, but cannot be found by *taking a train* somewhere outside you. The more you continue to search outside yourself for the love you believe you deserve or are capable of, the more you will lack faith in yourself.

We've already learned in this book that the reality of what you are is the Self of the Sonship, Christ, the Son of God. Christ is seen as the saving mind or the real Self of our wholeness. This is the love in you as well as the love within all whom you encounter daily. In the holy instant this Self is shared, and the ego-based mind will have no part of it. This is when we love, because Christ is Who we are, wholeness individualized but shared through love.

* * *

The reality of Christ within you is your holiness, and when

it is shared all thoughts of separation quickly fade away, which expands your vision of true reality. This is why your own holiness is so powerful, and by sharing it, you gain more strength and that strength reveals itself in relationships. How do we share this power of holiness? How do we come to share the Christ Mind we each are of?

It certainly doesn't mean running around town wearing special clothing and telling everyone you see, "Christ is within us all." No one will take you seriously, and you'll be seen as a pest. But your sincere simple acknowledgment of it is enough. When you notice this strength in another person you've been in a relationship with, or in a new relationship, and you sense their own genuineness, accept that as the Christ in them. They don't even have to be aware that you are sensing this in them. You will know if it's real because of the Christ in you, and you will know that you're not being fooled. Do you see the peace in this? The Holy Spirit gets you to this realization.

But if you perceive yourself as weak or limited compared to your partner's strength, you are concerned with your body as being who you are. You will be faithless. Try to see the strength in others you've been involved with as a compliment to your own positiveness and genuine spirit, which makes for a great relationship. If you simply cannot do this, then you are perceiving his or her gains as a threat for you to incur loss.

So ask yourself: When you think of another individual calling on God for help or for love, do you feel that your own calling to God can be just as strong? Also, when another's prayers seem to get answered, does this inspire you to see your own prayers getting the same treatment? Sure you do, you get inspired and you contemplate your prayers in your unique style of communicating within yourself.

What I mean is that deep within, you recognize glimpses of God as the Idea that runs your life positively, and your faith is strengthened due to your acceptance of God as an Idea each of us share.

But let me explain further by saying what you do find difficult to accept is that you along with the reality behind others, see the brotherhood itself as the One Idea of Creation. At first you may find this difficult to accept, but if you continue overlooking the body by looking well beyond it, the sense of it will sink in. You'll see a reflection of oneness more so than projections that make the images of bodily form.

Just like your Creator, you can give of yourself completely, wholly without loss and only gain. How do you give wholly? What does this mean?

For instance, try to see the light in the action taken by myself with the woman who wished I'd take up a hobby in collecting trains. My decision in the matter was rather simply to offer her a sincere opportunity to learn more about my passion with golf, and to try to see the game for the beauty in it.

When the time was right, I did, however, politely inform her that train collecting was not for me. She, of course, snorted that she could never consider "chasing a little white ball around some acreage." But this was fine with me that this understanding was brought forward in both our minds peacefully and conflict free. One of my proudest moments in handling something like this, I'll add, that very well could have gotten blown out of proportion.

But the fact of me as a train collector was never thought about again, ever! Without feeling of lack in either of us the idea was let go into oblivion like a helium balloon set free. Then it quickly dawned upon the two of us what a comical idea it really was, we made jokes out of it for a short while, and it wasn't too much longer after that when we parted as friends. No one was hurt and we both connected in lessons learned.

* * *

If you are leading a life of lack with scarcity thinking, your thoughts of peace and love will have no real meaning, simply because peace is replaced by conflict. You will strive to rise above scarcity, and all striving has conflict involved. Your conflicting focus will always be on gain versus loss and the worry thereof. Your awareness of perfect love becomes so fragmented that love is misunderstood.

But in the holy instant where there is no past or future to concern yourself with, only *now*, you move on to recognize the idea of love and are uniting this idea with the One Mind that *Thought* it. There is only one real Mind where duality doesn't exist. So in this sense, if you live within the *now*, or, a *holy instant*, how can you lose? But wait! Let's consider ego terms and its understanding of time: How long is a holy instant?

That is a good question proving your desire to lift the obscuring veil to your true light. The holy instant could be and usually is experienced starting off as a brief moment, and then on to two or three moments meeting together and so on. But as you move deeper to the center of One-mindedness the *instant* will lengthen and can be hours, days, weeks, years, or even the entire remainder of your time here on earth. You begin to *expect* your life to lead itself as you call the shots. Things will happen as expected while the Holy Spirit arranges the events, circumstances, chance meetings, and much more that give you your true heart's desire.

But in the holy instant lies your willingness, your understanding, and your full acceptance that the ego is nothing but a false idea of who and what you are. The holy instant overrides thoughts of the ego-based mind. Let's take a closer look.

* * *

Consider where your mind might be on a warm summer night when you suddenly notice that shooting star dart quickly across a calm, moon-lit, starry sky, maybe with the background sound of a distant train rolling down its tracks. In this *awe* of all that you sense, where are your thoughts of past and future?

Or, in that instant on a cool autumn afternoon while gently tramping through a colorful, sun-shadowed woods, when your ears first catch the echo of the hammering from a distant wood hen working on a hollow tree, with a background babbling brook, where are your thoughts of gain and loss?

Or, for you fellow golfers or imagined golfers, when your crisp five iron shot swishes down and through the sweet-smelling dew of a spring morning's turf just after sunrise, the ball spinning into the horizon and soon landing abruptly, with a short and tight dance of authority on the dance floor, a foot from the hole, where are your thoughts of conflict and fear then?

These types of moments by example, for however long they last, and by your choosing, are the mind activity of a holy instant. There is no clock time involved. It is nothing more than your reflection of love and truth which is total Oneness of mind. You've experienced eternity, your real Home.

The holy instant is effortless and becomes a lesson in holding onto Oneness of mind with all that exists as you reflect reality. This is where loss is unheard of, unreal, and only wholeness is your light of life. This is where all giving and receiving are appreciated as different aspects of the same thought, God's natural universal law. You have seen beyond time by overlooking it. You have forgiven your body and have realized your true existence. This is where fear cannot enter. Here is where you understand loves meaning, which is of the Christ Mind, the whole Son of God personalized.

In the holy instant is where the laws of wrong-minded ego-based thought cease to hold meaning any longer for you. It is where you come to know yourself by accepting your true free will as your reality—the only reality that exists. It's where you are not bound or limited by form. You've discovered the limitlessness that you are, by rising above guilt.

Chapter 19

An Exercise: God Is My Mind

Let's not confuse your true free will with your career, hobbies, or particular relationships. But let's do see the physical or material things in life that the world uses to define us, as often being the result of and that do compliment living a life of purpose.

We want to understand that when we accept responsibility for our relationships, career, volunteer activities, community involvements, public service, and so forth, our choice of having these functions as part of us is the result of our true free will. Your true free will is to lead the life that reflects who and what you truly are. This reflection of yourself is what helps to heal the world and is your part in the Atonement process.

Let's move forward in our minds, and see ourselves as the Creation of God, but from a vision you are capable of. You're capable of it because of your willingness to have it. We want to go beyond the body's eyesight. Attempt to go within your mind and visualize a place behind or beyond, based on which word suits you, all of your ego-based thoughts of being separate from God's Mind that have to do with the body.

For example, if you note a bundle of ego-based thoughts piled high with guilt, picture a veil or screen that these images have been projected onto, much like a home movie. *Behind* or just *beyond* the veil is your real thought system, your real unseparated all-loving you.

You will want to leave your bodily thoughts for a while. Yes, that's right; detach yourself from your body if you will, by using some imagination in seeing judgmental and attackful types of thoughts as nonexistent. This is where your knowledge of yourself is more than a body and is all that exists as eternally one.

The idea in this exercise ahead is deep but pleasant and is your springboard to real vision. You'll be lifted up. You will need to begin realizing why you have the power to call the shots in your life while here on earth. From this idea will the world open up to you and welcome you appreciatively. You'll begin seeing occurrences you have experienced in the past as now only faintly visible to you.

* * *

Let's try to envision a new kind of "projection." The ego will of course be involved because of your body, but not in control of it. Your body will become your happy servant. You won't be trying to get rid of what you don't want by seeing it outside yourself, instead you're wanting to see in the world only of what is in your real mind, God's Mind. You will only see what it is you want to occur in your life, because what you truly want is His Will. The goal is to join together with what you truly see rather than keeping it separate from yourself.

For example, if you feel you cannot or do not want to join with whatever it is you've been seeing and for whatever reason it might be, don't worry because it requires no validation. But do let go of it because it's not real in your mind. If you don't want it then it is an illusion and only undergoes the making of more ego-based needs, which are unreal and delays your healing of the split-mind.

If this is the case, you must surrender it by letting go and moving on to see what is in the world that you do want to join with, and then go forward to begin the journey of joining with it. By "join together," I mean being at-one with it in your mind to where it becomes you. This is what is real, unlike what the ego-based mind's way of the world has told you is only a fantasy. What you truly want is not fantasy; it is God's Will that you accomplish your goals.

In my own case it was becoming at-one with the literary field of fine, inspiring individuals who helped me make it possible to get my message to you. From prison I would see in my mind's eye my former lost self, my former career as a financial advisor fading away. Oh, sure, I'll always use what I've learned from the financial services industry for my own personal investing and so forth. But I've truly moved on and proceeded to do all that I could, using resources I could acquire only from outside of prison.

Discretely, with the help of my longtime friend, Ron Skeen, living in Florida, he was able to send me for study, directories, manuals, how-to books, and writing supplies. I'd write to publishers, editors, literary agents, and more, other authors, and anyone else, including the copyright holders of *A Course in Miracles,* the foundation of Inner Peace, who would all lend me helpful hints. I use the word "lend," because now I am able to "lend" my knowledge on to others. When that wasn't enough, I began to more and more visualize myself as already being a part of this fine group of men and women who truly wanted to help me.

I had become united with them regardless of how lost I had been in the past. Shakti Gawain's book, *Creative Visualization,* helped me to cross over the bridge to the truthfulness about myself.

When I'd receive letters in prison by regular mail from many of my Helpers, it was as though in their minds I'd been long overdue in joining them. I thought at first my incarceration hindered my pursuit, but then it was John Wilmer, a real estate author, who personally suggested to me that "life is full of experiences, some of which are not so pleasant."

My point is, you are what you truly say you are, regardless of what the ego wishes to declare for you. There is a fundamental difference between vision and the way you see with your body's eyes. But you must turn over the situation to the Holy Spirit—your true Helper—where Truth will run the course for you.

* * *

With all of these real thoughts in mind let's develop a dedication to the eternal, by considering this visualization practice, which I've used often myself and still do on a regular basis. It will soothe you with the knowledge of your oneness. It will be brought forward in your mind and will remain there, where you can incorporate it into a practice of your own developing or modifying based on your desires. Your own creation, if you will. The goal is to place yourself *at-one* with your purpose.

First you must contemplate this image, this visualization of reality:

See yourself as being *behind or beyond* your body. See that you are beyond the veil that holds the image of the stars and sun and all the galaxies entirely, past all you could ever possibly project. Now you see a seemingly familiar arc of golden light that stretches as you look into a great and shining circle.

The entire circle is filled with this light before your eyes. The edges of the circle now disappear and all that is inside of it is no longer contained at all. The light extends, expands, and covers everything, extending to infinity forever shining and with no break or limit anywhere. Within it everything is joined in perfect continuity. Nor is it possible that anything could be outside as there is nowhere without this light. This vision you have and which you are of, is the whole Son of God, and the Oneness that contains it is God the Father, Who holds your true free will.

Enjoy using this idea as you apply it to your personal life, relationships, your business or career goals, raising your children, etc. But use it as often as possible and preferably on some sort of regular routine by repeating these *words in meditation or prayer*:

"God is everything I see as I am the one Son of God. This is true because God *is* my mind due to me being *in Him. Thereby, my true free will is His Will.*"

As you tailor this practice to suit you, remember the goal is to realize that the idea applies to everything you see and to everyone. What you feel is real or can be seen as real if it were in the range of your sight. But it's only what you feel you truly wanted to see and become *one* with that could ever become real. Wishing is ego-based and is unreal.

Real vision is not limited to concepts such as "near" and "far"; to help you begin getting used to this idea, try to think of things beyond your present range, as well as those you can actually see, and apply the idea.

Real vision is not only unlimited by space and distance, but it does not depend on the body's eyes. The mind is its only source. To aid in helping you become more accustomed to this idea as well, devote some practice to this with your eyes closed if this makes you feel more comfortable. Be sure to use whatever subjects come to mind, including your relationships if you want, and looking within rather than without.

Let's repeat the words again:

"God is everything I see as I am the One Son of God. This is true because God *is* my mind due to me being in Him. Thereby, my true free will is His Will."

Chapter 20

A Bad Dream You Need Not Give in To

There is something to be said about taking responsibility when it's time to make a choice.

I found it in an old, yellowed, torn-apart, and folded inside-out newspaper, sitting up high on a shelf in a small closet that they called the library. This was at the prison that first held me upon my incarceration. After glancing at this article, I knew I'd appreciate it in some way, later. I gently ripped it out and stored it among my legal papers in my footlocker, with the intent to soon reflect on its message. So now I'll share this Ann Landers piece with you.

An old man on his deathbed spoke to the Lord. The man asked God if he could have a sneak preview of both Heaven and Hell, before passing on.

God said to the old man, who led a good, spiritual life, "come with me and I'll show you what hell is about." They entered a room where a group of people sat around a huge pot of stew. Everyone was famished, desperate, and starving, as well as looking malnourished. Each of them held a spoon that reached the pot, but each spoon had a handle so much longer than their own arm, that it could not be used to get the food into their own mouths.

After the old man had enough of this desperate scene, God said, "Come along, my son, follow me, and now I'll show you what Heaven is all about."

The man was surely hoping to see a sight much more improved than the suffering and turmoil that hell had owned. They entered another room, identical to the first, the pot of stew, the group of people, and the same long-handled spoons. But here in Heaven, everyone was blissful, positive, and well nourished.

"I don't understand," said the old man. "Why are they so happy here when they were miserable in the other room, called hell, where everything seemed to look the same?"

God smiled gently and said, "Ah, it's simple. Here, in Heaven, they know how to feed each other."

Little is asked of us to learn that love and fear cannot coexist within us at the same time. Try to realize that fear is all about the anxiousness of gain versus loss that needs its time restraints, where love needs none of this. In that same willingness to choose fear, you could rather choose love as all there is to see in your life, which includes your relationships, will be transformed from fear to joy. If this is the choice you give to the Holy Spirit, you will enable Him to give you everything you want.

* * *

Remember, what you want is well beyond fantasy wishing. It's in your willingness to *be* and to *have* all that you truly want, effortlessly and free of guilt. Any efforts opposite of your true willingness only bring on fear and keeps truth hidden where love will be missed.

The truth in what you really *want* is necessary for real vision, happiness, release from pain, and then you begin understanding that sin is only an image of fear and both are unreal. Sin is the illusion projected in the dream of separate identities that keeps you blocked from your true reflections. It's the error in thought that makes the separation, and it fragments more unreal thought, which gives the ego-based mind its false power to make projections and label what it is afraid of, "sin."

But it is the truth in you beyond fear that gives you the vision that sees yourself real and adhering to what you want. Wishes fade along with ego control over your reality. The body soon feels more comfortable there.

To reinforce this as your reality you must begin understanding and accepting that you are responsible for what you see. You can choose your own feelings, you decide on the goal you would receive. Try to see that everything happening to you is of your choosing; the abusive relationship *let go of* and on to your transformation of loving life rather than fear it, any longer. This is where you will begin receiving what is needed to accomplish your true free will upon your asking. There's truth in the statement, "Ask and you shall receive."

* * *

Don't deceive yourself any longer. It can't be difficult to realize that faith must be the opposite of no faith at all, where your worries, anxiety, unsettledness only add to your fears. This furthers your separated state of mind. Faith will remove any and all limitations in what you think you see. Having faith unites you in time to your purpose. How much time it takes is up to your faith in the Hold Spirit as He reverses your ties to fantasy, while bringing wholeness to you. You'll feel it arriving.

We often deceive ourselves that we're helpless in the face of our misfortunes, or we may see ourselves as victims to the actions of others we relate with. But not any longer when you simply acknowledge that you've been quite mistaken, and all effects of your mistakes will disappear. However, you must see within yourself that the Holy Spirit is ready, able, and waiting for your readiness level to be right, so He can undo all of this for you, and simply by your asking.

You can ask Him by making the simple statement to yourself only, and not to any other individual, that now you are both fully *willing and ready* to live your daily life, all your activities, around your true free will. By declaring this, you give the official indication to the Holy Spirit to begin His Task. Things will happen, keep your ears and eyes in tune, you'll begin to sense what may seem like intuitive thoughts arriving.

When you ask Him to begin, you'll have been given the understanding that having faith is to heal and is a sign you are reawakening, which mean you've accepted the Atonement within yourself. This means fantasy and wishing types of thoughts are being reversed to what it is you truly want. It's your choice, Heaven or Hell. One is real where what you *want* is given to you, the other is just a bad dream that you need not give in to.

Chapter 21

Is There Value in Intuition?

What does a life of total dedication to the truth really mean? How is it lived?

I like how M. Scott Peck MD, author of the famous book *The Road Less Traveled*, answers by saying, "It means leading a life of continuous and never-ending stringent self-examination. We know the world only through our relationship to it. Therefore, to know the world, we must not only examine it but we must simultaneously examine the examiner."

Before you can see your Inner Guide on His mission all around you or hear His many messages to you, you must turn on your receiver. You must accept the fact that your right-mind might be reaching out to tell you that you're either on the right track, or headed for further ego-based domination and control leading to conflict and turmoil in your life.

When you find yourself receiving thoughts like, "This rings a bell," or "something just doesn't seem right about this," or "I've a good feeling about her style, the way she speaks, and her honesty," then stop and listen to yourself for a while. Tune it in more closely if you must like a station on your radio that's certain but needs just a bit more clarity, because this is surely your intuition. But once you've tuned in, you should step back from the situation and reflect before making any rash decisions. Your ego could also be there waiting to take advantage of any anxious thoughts. If you have a hunch, don't go with your gut just yet, hang on, you'll need just a little more.

As much as I value intuition, it's not always so pure, or an unimpeachable knowledge from behind your own physicalness because of the ego's antics. But do release this hunch to the Holy Spirit asking that He filter it, and if the hunch is appropriate you will be directed in a fashion that is right for you as to how and when to proceed with action. Intuition can be influenced and entangled by your own selfish ego-based wishing in order to gain something over others. You should know why you are reacting to a particular person the way you are before you allow a hunch to dictate your actions. Something about the current situation might be stirring up a recollection. But who knows what it may be?

You may have an adverse reaction to a man named Ralph, for no better reason than that being the name of the grouchy old man across the street who terrorized the kids in the neighborhood when you were growing up. You haven't known a Ralph you've liked since. That's hardly a good reason not to go to work with someone by that name or not to hire a car mechanic named Ralph.

At first when the intuitive notion arises try to open it up and learn from it. Try to recognize and respect it. Don't ignore or dismiss it, but don't follow it blindly either. Put some real vision into it. Think of yourself like a dog who hears a noise in the distance. You stop, become alert, and turn your ears in the direction of the noise. By doing that, you'll be tuning on your intuition receptors, and *tuning out* wishful ego-based thinking.

* * *

If you can see yourself as the whole Son of God where you operate by the Christ Mind—that infinite extending circle of golden light with no edge lines which we visualized earlier— then it will be impossible for you to be driven by events outside yourself. How can anything real be outside the infinite? It's also impossible that occurrences could come your way that have never been your choice.

Your own power of decision is what determines every situation in which you find yourself, and it's not by accident or luck. There are no chance meetings, because you are always in the right place at the right time whether you realize it or not. Not a single accident is possible within the real universe, which is not the projected image you call the physical universe. All that is real is of the unseparated thought behind the veil that holds the projection. Whatever is outside is nothing except that which can only be recognized with fear and pain, and having something to do with the body. *You,* as God's Child, do not possess fear or pain ever, but your body will choose to do so.

The suffering and pain is based on your decision that sin is real, and had been all along as a goal to live outside yourself. Your body is *not* part of the real Universe where true joy and love exist. Your body can, however, be an experience of such elation. The real unique you that are united with the Christ Mind are in control of the power of decision that determines our true joy. This is the gift given you through the Holy Spirit so you can give to yourself and give to others from within yourself. This is true extension.

Therefore, with this knowledge be certain to give Him your willingness to be all you can be. Hold this within you by keeping the world of your true vision rather than how others might persuade you, regardless of well-intended but misinformed people in your life, when you truly know what is right for you. Thank them kindly and be on your way without looking back.

But beware: if you give away what you sincerely behold, in exchange for a separated thought process, everything you truly see goes with it. In the holy instant is where you maintain the truths you see, and the truth knows God's Universe.

* * *

Don't you truly know when you're not being completely honest with yourself? When you feel the untruth of that situation you're feeling it from within the universe, but your dishonesty is outside the realm of whom and what you are. Or, we can say it is outside the universe, so how can it be real?

There is power in your *wanting* a situation to arise because the universe is where the world you want is given to you but first you must recognize and then accept the power of your wanting.

Your *wanting* becomes your strength and any wishing only weakens you. When you want something, you expect it to arrive, but there's no truth at all in wishing. My own grandmother always told us right up to her death at age ninety-five: "Don't *wish* upon a star, but do *want* what is beyond it."

What you *want* is truthful and sustains you. Thereby, accept what you want and allow it to come to you. It's yours. With this strength you can now perceive that your wishes have only *made* a world you must let go of, so you can begin *creating* the world you truly want. It's never too late, because in this instant, *now,* is the only time there is in the real world.

The world we see around us can be considered a witness that says, "You are only correct in what your body's eyes see." But think about this. *What* is the witness? It is nothing but a projected image and cannot possibly see the real world beyond form. A projection on a movie screen only has vision on the screen. It has no capabilities for real seeing.

For centuries we've been coaching the testimony of this witness, teaching it how to see things. As it projected back to us through time we listened and convinced ourselves that what we've been seeing all along is real. We did this to ourselves by making a projection of our lives. Likewise, all of our lives are separate, individual, and different projected images of each other and of the world, where much of it is chaos. We've even defined this projection of separateness down to *no two fingerprints alike.*

If we see and believe the sworn testimony of these projections that began at the separation, then we all see a different and separate vicious circle for reasoning. This is not what was given us, but it is the illusion we made and gave to ourselves, while we continue passing it along. But because you accepted it from yourself, your projection of your brother/sister is making his own illusion of his own body as you see him in your projection. In other words, you have made your brother/sister into the image you wish him to be. This is what started the second hand of time ticking away, and it keeps the illusion being the illusion you wish to have.

So now is the time where we must be willing to replace illusion by looking beyond it to the truth of what truly is there.

It's what you truly want. So how can you proceed? It's simple. When you choose to begin seeing the change necessary and focus on your goals of true "wanting" rather than wishing for things to be different, only then will you see it reflected in your world and naturally reciprocated in your relationships.

Chapter 22

When Vision Is Denied for Wishing

In a discussion with a friend of mine he had stated that it wasn't necessary for him to offer his willingness to the Holy Spirit. He concluded by saying he has always prayed seriously directly to God and that this was enough. If this is your way of thinking then that's great, because God and the Holy Spirit are one and the same. The concept of the Holy Spirit helps us in a concrete manner see a communication link between ourselves and our creator that helps give a sense of oneness that the concept and beliefs in duality have taken from us.

If unsettled and insecure thoughts have entered your mind, take a close look at what "offering your willingness" really means.

Consider that your separated thoughts of wishing things were different have been constructed so that you can be saved from what haunts you. Maybe you'll finally get what you want is what you begin to think.

The ego-based mind is a separated idea that tells you particular things are possible for you as Son of God without the Will of the Father. But we're learning that His Will is never separate from your own. The ego-based idea of this is your replacement for His Will, where it becomes your revolt against that which is eternal.

The ego's false idea is that you must take your free will seriously and is separate from what God wills for you. The ego's way of thinking tells us that God's Will is some sort of special ministry with studies, diplomas, and doctorates to obtain, and that this "Will of God" is not suited for everyone. For instance, a "man of the cloth" is seen as "doing God's Will." But doesn't the world have such meaningful words to where our choice is to understand them as they were designed?

What I really mean is, we must remember one all important fact which the ego refuses to accept, and which because of this may at first thought or so, make it not so clear for you to comprehend. It's that, what God has willed for you actually creates in yourself His Will to be yours. In other words, you have willed His Will for yourself. You've done this naturally because His Will is what you truly want. Without inheriting God's Will you are lacking, scarcity thinking haunts you, and you also note an entire world as a whole lacks likewise. This is why the world you see around you can never be whole. Whatever the ego-based mind makes can never know wholeness. But it can collectively accommodate its many fragments and call that whole.

Now you should understand why the ego-based mind's thought system believes you can't have the whole pie, but that pieces are to be shared. Its cop-out is "to want is selfish" and it's better to wish. But when we wish for something we're leaving room for doubt. The ego needs to keep you doubting for its mere survival.

But on the other hand what you truly want gives you joy because it's what God wants, and I assure you He always gets what He wants, because it is His Will. Anything other than God's Will is clearly wishful thinking. It is the doubtful thinking that makes the projections of this world.

Self-made wishing is not an aspect of the holiness that abides you, but it is the fearful idea that is responsible for the making of church doctrine. It becomes wishful religious dogma that we enshrine upon an altar of worship, so that we may one day gain Heaven. Since time began we've developed such a fear of loss that we fear Heaven might not be achieved. We're so separated in thought we can't see that we've never left our Divinity.

But amazingly so, anything that may dare to threaten this dogmatic approach seems to attack the faith we wish to enshrine. The nature of the ego-mind which is a false nature makes you tend to think that by recognizing this fear tactic means you are faithless. Rather, let's see it as knowledge of the truth and acknowledge this as your faith.

The Holy Spirit will give you faith in your own holiness, which is the same holiness of Christ, where truth is your real vision. This truth about you is your altar; it's your real mind behind the veil that holds the image of your body. It's where your willingness to extend your reality exists.

* * *

Your willingness is not in any other device outside your reality such as in doctrines, dogmas, sacrifices, or penances. A true willingness is within. It's in your heart, the wholeness of mind you truly are. This is where your own natural gifts abide, but you have placed idols ahead of what is real. These idols, which are nothing more than the will of your unruliness which seem to preach to you what must occur, what you must do, and how to do it, until you decide to give up or let go of wishing and of idols. The Holy Spirit asks of you to make room for what you don't understand and not to dwell on it.

We're afraid to accept we are of the Mind of God. We're afraid to look this far beyond what the body has taught us. Try to be willing just for an instant to leave your altar—your mind—clean of what your past has placed on it. What truly sits there now? Is it the whole naked Truth?

It's okay for you to only see the truth of who you are, regardless of ego arrogance that will try to intrude. That truth is the infinite vision of Christ. See the holy instant as the recognition of who you are and all that you are. This only arrives through real vision and not from judgment. This is why you are holy and not from standards set by outside sources.

Try to begin seeing that when you suspend all judgment you are looking within yourself, clearly without obstruction and seeing what is truly there. It is a whole because it is without judgment from yourself, and the world's judgment doesn't penetrate you. Throw all judgment aside in this holy instant, now. Your non-condemning attitude will uncover your true free will, where wishes can't hold a candle to your true capabilities.

Undoing errors that dream up your wished-for fantasies is not your task, but it is up to you to welcome your Teacher so He can lead you to the faith and desire that go hand in hand with what it is you truly want. There is no true desire or faith that serves as a foundation for fantasy.

* * *

It should be plain to see that wishing and guessing through hunches is how the ego-based mind deals with what it thinks it wants. This is why part of you believes you must strive toward achievement. This can be stressful and the breeding ground for anxiety, and backs up the rule of "no pain, no gain."

Faith in the unreal leads to making adjustments to reality so it may fit the goal of fear of guilt. We make a goal of wishing to make a reality of the unreal. Why do we do this? Because we think we must construct what we wish for at all cost. If we see the reality of it not being truthful, we proceed to build a foundation for it by adjusting what is real, thus making an unreal situation to satisfy the wishful thinking, but with guilt, doubt, and fear hanging over like cloud cover. It's the process of obscuring your true light.

As example, this brings to mind a scenario some years ago in my mind when I first began giving seminars and hosting workshops to groups of fifty or better, in my practice as a financial advisor. I'd worry before each session, but was also surprised and didn't have a clue how I naturally made folks feel at ease with my down-to-earth demeanor, and would get a few laughs or so that helped gel the group.

I was pleased at how I was able to capture the audience effortlessly. That was until I decided to enroll in a motivational speaking course, guaranteeing me to improve by changing several things in my style of speaking.

I soon discovered that the aggressive techniques and strategies they taught made me feel uncomfortable, and I knew it wasn't right for my audiences. When I experimented with my new style, the results were poor. I learned I was not intended to be a motivational speaker and that the ranting and raving this school taught was not in my heart.

I immediately reverted back to trusting that my own creativity would always be there for me when I needed it, and I quit worrying about it. This experience cleared the doubt on my path and my own acknowledgment came forward in the fact that God is doing the creating for me and it's up to me to extend it. Wishing plays no part in creativity.

* * *

When real vision is denied for wishing, confusion of *cause and effect* will be inevitable. Your purpose in wishing will be to keep hidden true *cause and effect* which is one, not two, by making *effect* to appear as a *cause*. We could say the ego always sees things opposite or upside down to reality, and that is why we often put the "cart before the horse," so to speak. This gives effect a false independence that enables it to be regarded as standing by itself and capable of serving a *cause* for the events and appearances you *wish* to have. It's fantasy.

In this sense you are making your own creator or attempting to be the Father and not the Child. As the Son of God, you are truly the *effect* of a *cause* which you can never truly deny or substitute. Nothing has effects without a cause, and to confuse this is merely making *cause and effect* into duality, and this results in your failing to understand what you truly are. You'll lead a wishful way of life and will continue to look around the corner for fantasy. You will never accomplish what you truly want in life with this approach.

It will help your own transcending into the real world if you'll recognize you didn't create yourself. Nothing created by your true Creator could ever have a dictatorship or demanding-type influence over you, especially where relationships are concerned.

If you think what you made by projection can tell you what you see and feel, and then place your faith in its ability to do so, you will be denying your Creator and believing you made yourself.

If you think the world you made has the power to make you into what it wishes, then you are confusing yourself with your real Source—God—resulting in guilt along with fear sadly becoming what you face in your life while you are here. Certainly not what you *want*.

Chapter 23

Guilt as the Ultimate Punishment

Both in their late seventies I thought it was great the last time my parents drove seven hours round trip to visit me in prison. It was such a pleasant time for the three of us, considering yours truly still having time to serve on my sentence.

I was surprised how they conversed all the while maintaining a moderate sense of humor throughout the visit and about what I was doing now to earn my sanity and safety in these volatile conditions. Upon preparing to end the visit and get on the road for home, my father seriously asked me a question he'd prolonged with a humorous stint. He asked, "Jim, how's your relationship with God been?"

I hesitated only briefly but firmly answered with a slightly positive grin, responding to his humorous hint, but giving my dad the serious answer he was looking for, by saying, "We've never had a difference of mind."

They both chuckled in agreement and that was all that Mom and Dad needed to hear from their oldest of six, sending them on a drive home with a good feeling of hope, the hug from my mother and her teary-eyed positive smile, and firm handshake with a pat on the shoulder followed by his own quick manly hug, was enough to send me back into the prison house, where I'd return to my mission and regimen of getting through all of this, with the sight of one day rejoining society.

Is there one thing in your life you'd like to feel more at peace about? For me it's still the haunting of my incarceration. Is there something for you that possibly has you reacting negatively? Try to make a mental decision to release it, letting it go, forgiving you for being in the predicament. Often we need to picture what it is we can do now, in this instant, to move forward and create a process that you can continue. Let the Holy Spirit know your intent.

Certainly, being the Spirit of God, which means He is the trueness of yourself, meaning, He is you, the Holy Spirit already knows your intentions. But by acknowledging to Him with the firmness in my dad's handshake, tell Him what you truly want to see in this world, and you will begin reflecting that state of mind. This is how you get closer to the center of your true eternal light.

* * *

While we're here in the dream of life it's our choice to either make it meaningful or live a nightmare. Which do you choose? I've learned it must consist simply of embracing the responsibility of my true free will, while I face head on the many obstacles which can be transformed into learning experiences.

Even with much interference along the way you can enjoy your task. There may be times that the types of work you're forced to do are not so satisfying. But if it is seen as a stepping-stone to where you want to be, then there is surely joy in that aspect of the task. The nature of what we enjoy connects us with the moral order of wholeness. It's the One-mindedness with God and His Son in wholeness with God and His Son in wholeness—Christ, which is the moral order we each behold.

The workbench, the kitchen counter, the computer station, the classroom, the welder's torch my father held until his retirement, the writer's desk, or any other work space can be your altar. There is intrinsic meaning to work well done and it is appreciated as a reflection of who you are, which extends joy on and on.

But if we fail to grasp this right-minded notion and that of our singularity, we become shallow individuals. The guilt that this shallowness holds keeps us from the depths of our reality. We'll never find it easy to see the center of ourselves. Something will most always seem to be missing, as the ego-based mind thinks it helps us to find the completeness we yearn for.

I had to learn to deal with this in prison, when I had nothing to do but the most mundane chores I was assigned. Shortly after entering prison I literally stumbled into *A Course in Miracles*, and I had never seen another copy while in prison. Likewise, when I discretely asked others, no one else had ever heard of it. Due to its extremely deep and abstract content, the *Course* would not be a popular study in prison, much as the Bible is. My point is, somewhere deep within me there was a spark or flicker of light that has brightened me with my relationship with the *Course*, and it has become my life study, along with the Bible. A miracle.

* * *

I feared that the desultory prison life would begin to affect my habits, discipline, and mind. With my time in prison I set myself on a strict regimen. I forced myself to get up early at 4:30 each morning just after the 4 o'clock inmate count, so I could meditate and begin writing and studying. I'd organize my day into various projects like reading, writing, preparing outlines that led to chapter drafts of several of my books, more writing, and more meditation.

When I first arrived in prison a case manager told me, "Just settle in and accept it. This is where you live now. Don't think about home. You must learn to consider this your home."

But my constant study of *A Course in Miracles,* which also led to a finer interpretation of the Bible, the way I see it, and other spiritual teachings, convinced me to do just the opposite of the case manager's advice. I was facing into the ugly teeth of a *ten-year* prison term and the thought of this alone hurt more than I can ever begin to explain. I absolutely did not want to "adjust" to prison life. Nor did I want to call it home.

The *Course* has inspired me to drive myself as hard as I could while in prison and I did so with pure pleasure. As I write this book all the original notes were compiled while in prison, so you may catch glimpses of present-tense writing even though I've translated it into past tense. I can say that my entire days were consumed with writing, studying, doing my job in the prison chow hall, exercising, and tutoring a few illiterate inmates. I seldom allowed myself to participate, nor did I desire any of the so-called recreation, which is a breeding ground for gang activity and trouble. As far as I was concerned, I was on a mission to put this material in your hands and to extend my thought. But I'll be straightforward and honest as I say, deep inside me, the inspiration came to me from my fear of losing myself.

At work in the chow hall for a while, I operated the dishwasher, and working next to me as we loaded tray after tray onto a conveyer belt, was a serial murderer, who enjoyed the general population since being released from many years of *super maximum* security.

Brandon saw joy in working the dishwasher room. This is how we became acquainted and I considered him one of my "dudes," a term used to describe a friend but still with caution. Getting acquainted was one thing in prison, but getting close was not recommended. By the way, my dude Brandon, described *supermax* as unbearable solitary confinement, where even one's mail is read through a window under supervision. Brandon described, too, without getting gruesome, the murders he committed, alone, out of a jealous rage over his wife. She was one of the four victims that sentenced him to *life without a chance of parole.*

Our work consisted of placing dirty food trays through the dishwasher in one end and out the other side. We made it a team effort. The most challenging part of the job for me was going over in my mind the writing assignments I gave myself the night before, as I loaded tray after tray onto the conveyer belt, while my dude, Brandon, stacked the clean trays on the other end.

That particular job in the chow hall lasted about three hours each morning during and after breakfast, and then I was on my own for the rest of the day to my task at hand on my daily regimen, while also watching over my shoulder for sneaky foul and aggressive attack.

* * *

I'd always used my time on prison work to think how I might one day begin to live again, and, ironically, what I was learning confirmed my experience right there in the dish room. I found that any type of work can be significant and satisfying when you give it a purpose and accept it only for what it is.

I could see that the empty hours sucked the life directly out of many prisoners. They allowed their bunk areas to become dirty and sloppy, they ignored simple hygiene like keeping a clean washcloth, a clean cup for drinking water, or even having a toothbrush at all. Some of the ones with false teeth would leave them without a case, sitting on the dirty concrete floor next to their bunk. If they were on a work detail they hung around talking, usually about their resentment toward others they labeled "snitches," and other enemies, as well as the prison system itself. But each day I'd always look at the previous day as being in the past and gone. Like it was only a dream, a bad one at that.

Those who didn't have work assignments at all were mostly inmates with life sentences, who'd refuse to work and had lost all hope. I tried to keep this thought of them in a present moment.

I'd see their entire days spent on their bunks, half-dazed staring into the air, trying to escape into the emptiness of their thoughts. They were sleeping their lives away. I'd come to understand what a severe punishment prison is, and that is why I gave others a sense that I was there to listen to them in a discrete manner, if they'd like.

While prison does take a piece of one's life away, society's ultimate punishment is taking a person's whole life through guilt, and it finds its way into everyday existence even for those who have never been to prison.

Upon leaving prison I'd hoped to return to relationships, ones that ended abruptly due to my incarceration. Some I was able to rejoin and others I had to let go of, only because they were too far gone. But with my time spent in prison with minimal touch to the outside world, I'm seeing relationships in a new and different light, both family and friends.

We wish to have friends or even to fall in love, and, then, the special relationship is formed. But isn't it more so an attempt at getting something? It's the completion of something we seem to feel is missing in our lives, and which we strive to gain at all cost. But beyond this attraction to gain, already lies our completion. It's simply the complete love of our Creator. He is Who we are. There can be nothing else, because Oneness of all that exists requires nothing else other than including you and me.

One is one and cannot be more or less. This Oneness is only love, and love is truth which is all there is to real life which is fully given and fully received. There is nothing to be considered special at all in this unlike the ego's claim to its own specialness and its search for the same, which, of course, never can seem to be any more special than itself.

Chapter 24

The Chains of Guilt

In seeking to gain a single thing, the ego in us likes to use its specialness to keep the giver bound to itself through guilt. I mean, the ego-based mind wishes that the giver never hold specialness greater than its own.

The ego-mind will not lead you to a relationship without some form of anger it has been harboring. It believes this helps to gain friends through mutuality. But, of course, the ego in us will have a difficult time owning up to this. If it does, it will surely add: "What else is there to talk about?"

Think for a moment about the things we hold onto, the unsettledness, the distrust in the world we despise, the conflict of opinion. It always seems to be something with the economy, the markets, greedy politicians, our rebellious teenagers, corruption, and even bad weather brings us an unsettled topic for discussion. We use such agreeable conflict to motivate conversation at a cocktail party, family gatherings, church socials, or any type of gathering where we wish to fit in with others. This seems to be our way for getting acquainted.

The ego's main attraction is making guilt, but it always seems to attract through love and will stay clear of another it thinks may see its "guilt-enforcing" strategy. The ego fears its façade might be exposed for its *artificiality*. If you begin to notice this in yourself simply look closely at it while shedding true light on it. You do this much like you would glare at your child when catching him pulling a nasty prank. Notice, then, how it makes you feel.

If you feel guilty because you caught yourself thinking inappropriately, then you've allowed the ego to sneak in the back door on you. In this case, simply acknowledge the ego's hold on you and release it to the Holy Spirit. Be sure to accept it, and then, let it go.

The more you practice acknowledging the ego's illusive presence working at taking over your thoughts, the less the ego will feel it can prevail over you. It will get careless with its thought control and you'll feel some frustration and edginess that you can't pin its starting point. The reason you can't explain its occurrence is because it's nothing but illusion just like any other past. So go forward by acknowledging this to yourself, too.

* * *

One thing you can be certain of, the ego will not quit trying to control your thoughts through projection until it dies. This is when your body no longer breathes oxygen. But this is okay, too, because by your true self accepting the ego as the pest, you stay in charge of how you view the world. You will remain in control similarly as you would with your child pulling the prank. Your true thought system knows it breathes eternal air, and this knowledge in itself keeps a tight leash on the ego.

By understanding this while you're here in this world you'll easily turn the ego's antics over to your personal Comforter and Helper. He will use time to free you from guilt, and how much time necessary is always based on your willingness to get rid of it and your readiness to move forward, in understanding that errors will still occur. But you will experience minimal discomfort in the process, if any.

The more you recognize your attraction for guilt and what it does to add more agony into your life, you can stop making it real and be more apt to surrender it freely and automatically. You will naturally notice it right away and know what to do.

I agree, it is tough to let go of what holds value. But why do we value guilt? Because we really never learned what it is, and we have also judged it as a weapon to weaken others and ourselves. Why do we wish to weaken ourselves? We don't, but the ego-based mind that dreams of separation does weaken you so it can gain control. We actually go to extremes of even abusing ourselves to make us appear as having strength. This kind of judgment and condemnation rather than vision has been our wrong-minded approach for gaining ever since the "bad apple" was taste tested by Eve.

But let's discuss you, *now*. As you learn to truly accept your *wanting* of real vision versus making judgments all day long, you will naturally shift your perceptions and thoughts over to a *majority holding* of right-mindedness. How do you begin this shift? How do you make right-mindedness the major shareholder of your thought system?

It's quite easy, once you begin asking yourself some serious questions, that neither Eve nor Adam back at the symbolic Garden of Eden ever considered. Do you want to feel guilty and, why would you want others to feel the same ugliness? If that is not enough then honestly ask, again, "What am I afraid of?"

* * *

The ego-based mind's mission is trying to maintain and increase the value of guilt as its main investment in its portfolio. But it does so in such a way that we don't recognize the toll it takes on us. The ego's thought system has a golden rule that says *"doing to others what you think you have escaped."* It wishes no one do well with a disguise that wishes them the "best of luck."

Consider, what is it about a part of us that likes to see others punished or suffer? We often say "serves them right" when an error has been made.

When I was indicted by a grand jury and later sentenced to *ten years* in prison, a local newspaper ran an article with a bold headline that told its readers I was "Brought to My Knees" along with a photograph of me in handcuffs standing before an angry judge.

We have hidden within us something that likes to see the *dirty laundry* of others. We find safety in this. There's even a famous classic song about our desire to witness "dirty laundry." Yet, the survival of the ego-based mind depends on the belief that you are exempt from your own dark side being exposed.

Try to consider why in the example of myself that an article had never been run about my desire to make whole of my mistake, as well as my willingness to help others by example not fall into the same pit that led to my poor decision making? Is this a cop-out? To the ego it is. Am I bitter toward the media? Of course not, for that would be the ego sneaking in the back door on me.

The ego will counsel you that if you will host its guilt so that you'll be permitted to direct your anger outward for your own projection purposes, which it believes to be its show of strength. The problem with that is, the ego always feels it needs to be protected by images. This is why we seek out an endless array of special relationships for our endless fragmenting ego-based needs. We seek support of others in the idea of our own anger being directed outward for our own safety.

As we gain the justification of others, we think we feel stronger in that our anger is now permissible. But this is what chains us to guilt, and this is what the Holy Spirit must unlock so that we come to know our own holiness. Can we place chains around God? This is what you try to do when you chain yourself or your relationships to guilt.

Chapter 25

Your Willingness to See Guilt as Illusion

The ego-based mind instructs us to make relationships based on its idea of sacrificing itself. Being a sacrificial lamb gives the ego a feeling of worthiness and a larger-than-life attitude, but with both being real.

The sacrifice the ego-mind invents is actually the root of its bitter resentment. The thinking seems to concern "all that has been given" to someone else. For example, does this sound familiar in others or in yourself: "After all I've done for her, now she stabs me in the back. Ruined me!" or, "I gave up my career for him only to find him involved with another woman. He doesn't realize how well I treated him."

The ego-based thought system is confusing because it thinks in contradictory terms. For example, it will acknowledge reality as it wishes it to be, and on the other hand is aware that no one could interpret the attack of another as being an act of love. Yet, to make someone feel guilty certainly is attack, but the ego will delude itself to think otherwise. The one who seems to hang onto guilt expects to be attracted to it.

Let's clearly look at it this way:

Many of us have been in abusive relationships, where we seem to be attracted to what we really don't want. Each party seems to think they have sacrificed something to the other which they both regret, then hating the other for it. Yet, one or both of them thinks it is what they want. If one leaves the situation it usually results in the other placing blame for feeling victimized.

What we must understand here, is that they are not in love with each other, but are obsessed with the sacrifices made.

Because of the sacrifices you demand of yourself, you may be demanding that your partner accept the guilt and sacrifice herself, as well. It is quite impossible to forgive this scenario, because the ego believes that to forgive her would be to lose her. The ego must have this control in order to attack and not to forgive and will blame someone or something to ensure guilt as the backbone of its relationships. We see these relationships everywhere, but they like to hide in disguise as the loving-couple image that they try so hard to portray.

While this is not a book on alcohol or drug abuse, specifically, such substance abuse will often reveal the ugliness of the ego through guilt and jealousy tirades. Additionally, how often are a few drinks considered for a "loosening up" on that special first date, and, then, many times the evening ends up a night in hell?

The ego simply cannot have a relationship other than strictly with a body. It's in this way that the ego wishes for love and happiness and is why it never concerns itself with what the mind thinks.

* * *

The reality and endless bliss the mind offers you holds no importance to the ego-based mind. As long as the body is there to perceive its sacrifice the ego is content and judges the mind as being too private.

But as much as the ego denies the mind, it also surely realizes its existence. If it didn't realize the mind for the power it has, then why wouldn't it just have a relationship with a designer mannequin? If this question brought forward a slight smile or chuckle in you, then you've experienced the Holy Spirit shining some light onto your thoughts. If so, casually accept it.

Although the ego is aware of the mind, ideas are basically of no concern except as they bring the body of another closer together, or to push it away. These are the terms in how it judges ideas as either good or bad. No vision involved.

For instance, whatever it is she can do to make him feel guilty and hold him there for her gain is judged as good by herself. On the other hand, what would release him from guilt she judges as bad, because it would be a threat that the mind might be stronger than the body? The ego will fret even further in the fact that he has caught on to her manipulation and may leave.

But keep in mind that what I have just replayed is evident in the relationship with yourself and how you treat yourself, just as it is in the special relationship with couples.

The late Abraham Maslow had written and spoke of guilt being associated to pain. "We know that physical pain is desirable, because it tells us that part of our body is hurting; similarly, intrinsic guilt is healthy, because it communicates that we have betrayed or violated our higher nature in some way."

* * *

From its own suffering to its own sacrifices is how the ego-based mind will interpret its love in relationships. This is how the world has been made. At its altar we take our vows to unite one another by accepting these sacrifices as the price for togetherness. The mindset of this union seems to be a "devotion to hard work" at the relationship. But do we even know *what* it is we work at?

When anger arrives and the fear of loneliness sets in, each seeks relief in guilt by increasing it in the other. They each, then, seem to always be attacking and wounding each other, perhaps in little ways that unconsciously build up to become a conscious pile of mental prison rocks. The emotions then get out of hand quite often.

If you become angry with a person you're involved with, you can be certain you have gone to work at forming the *special relationship*, and the ego-based mind is controlling it. Anger is its blessing, guilt is its builder. Anger takes on many forms, but it will not deceive those for long who have a keen sense that love does not inspire guilt in any fashion.

Think for a moment about when you are angry. Isn't it an attempt to blame or make someone feel guilty? This attempt is the only basis the ego-based mind accepts for the special relationship. This is why it feels special. It is special for your ego, nothing more. Guilt is the only need the ego has to find specialness, and as long as you identify with it, then guilt will remain attractive to you. You think you need it.

"Wait a minute," I hear you saying, and then asking an all-too-important question we must address: "Why should we not feel special or be told we're special? After all, it brings joy and isn't this what love and life is all about?"

The joy which specialness brings doesn't last. It's artificial and is a great cover-up for our main source of guilt. Which is what? It's the guilt that has made a projection of the flesh we hide behind. The guilt of separation from the Mind of God. And, the guilt for not accepting that the separation isn't real.

So does this mean we should not honor people for special doings and events that may even help mankind, or simple birthdays, anniversaries, holidays, and other special occasions? Absolutely not! You should participate in all of this. But your understanding of what specialness really entails is your communication with the Holy Spirit. It is an acknowledgment that the ego-based mind doesn't control you because it's *not* real.

Try to remember this: is being with a body communication? If you think it is, you will feel guilty about communication and be afraid to hear the Voice of the Holy Spirit. He is in your mind, and your fear comes from communicating with what you can't see with the body's eyes. It's the "doubting Thomas" in you that makes you fear God and real love.

The Holy Spirit can't teach you through fear. How can you expect Him to communicate with you when you believe that communicating from your heart would make yourself alone, or subject to loss? It's clearly crazy to believe that by communication you will be abandoned. Many believe their minds must be kept private or they'll not be found at "face" (body) value, and they will lose each other. It is this union of bodies that keeps minds apart. But ask yourself, do bodies know how to forgive? They can only do as the mind gives direction to the brain to begin its activity. A projection in the dream of form.

It only takes a little spark or tiny flicker of willingness to communicate, the light attracting more communication to it where guilt begins to be overcome. Why is only a little spark of light necessary? Because the part of the mind that slipped into the dream of separation and guilt is *so much* similar.

Chapter 26

Salvation Is Your Choice

My goal has been that by now you should be understanding that holiness and salvation do not just magically arrive to you unannounced from somewhere "out there," but rather, both are the *miracle* that have always been within you.

The temptations we have come from nothing more than not knowing all we need to know about ourselves while in this world. We're afraid to open our eyes to the fact that all we truly need is within us. We surely feel the guilt, but likewise with salvation, we're not seeing it as being in our minds that easily. I mean, we think we must work at attaining it and make sacrifices to receive it as a reward.

Guilt is solely an invention, and it is then constructed from the tiny segment of mind that dreams it is separate, and blankets our real vision of salvation. Both are in the same place except the latter is real and is of the whole mind that does not recognize the tiny portion that dreams. By understanding this in times of confusion and despair, if you will revert to the real thought of wholeness rather than wasting away in the unreal, in an instant you are healed, which is to be saved. There is no effort involved in gaining salvation, but it is a choice you make over guilt.

However, in this fact there is a seeming cost by your acceptance of the idea. It will terribly trouble your ego to see that nothing outside yourself has the capability to save you from anything. Likewise, nothing outside of yourself can give you peace.

The ego-based mind will use religious dogma to try to prove you wrong. But please keep in mind, here, we're not dogging religion, it is the ego-based mind that has constructed the dogma for its control. It's not religion itself, it is in the choice we make in how we honor religion as either within or outside ourselves. Remember, nothing outside yourself has the power to control your faith or disturb your peace of mind, and all that abides in you can only love because it's whole.

By accepting the truth and holding it in as a part of your *essence,* or, *being,* which is all that creates you, and how you approach this separated world of projected images, your faith places you in charge of the universe. There are no outside forces. The whole Son of God—the Sonship operated by the Christ Mind—forever accompanies you as your free will is brought to lights. Didn't Jesus try to get this message to us when he spoke of being "The Way, the Truth, and the Life?"

This is where you always belong and is not a role you can sometimes play when you think you need to be tough or dominant or positive, because that would only mean the ego has snuck in the back door on you. Where you belong is your reality.

The illusion of guilt is hurtful. It's a self-inflicted wound from separated thought that is unreal and needs healing. God placed the remedy—Truth—for your well-being where it can help. Through guilt is the manner in how your mind hallucinates as you dream of time, space, and form being all separate from your Source. God wants you to be healed of the split-mind and that's why He kept the *Way* of healing where the need for it is in *Truth*, which is His *Life*, and is what Jesus spoke of.

All along throughout time we have tried to do just the opposite, making every attempt, however distorted and fantastic it might seem, to separate healing from sickness (guilt) as a reality. We've made it our purpose to always be ensuring that healing doesn't take place, whereas God's purpose by use of His Holy Spirit is to ensure it does. But what we so desperately need to bring into our reality is that God's Will and ours are actually the same.

How so? you ask. Because God wants us to heal from the illusion that we are separate from Him, which is to awaken and be free of guilt. Likewise, we don't want to be sick where we lack joy. By accepting this healing thought, wouldn't you say your mind and your life is in agreement with God? Of course so, and healing is currently taking place in the *Way*, the *Truth*, and the *Life* of your Source.

* * *

Here is an exercise I recommend you practice on a regular basis. Try to make it a routine, by repeating the following idea to you. You want to become at-one with these words in the form of prayer or meditation.

"My salvation comes from me. It is embedded within my true essence and cannot come from anywhere else."

Once you have become used to the idea, try to review in your mind some of the external places you've looked for salvation, at any particular period in your life. But be sure not to judge it by condemning yourself; instead, observe it as only an error.

This particular thing or number of things may have been in other people, in possessions, in various situations and events, or in self-concepts that you wished to make real.

For example, here's one of these things for me because I've had a few in the twenty-five years I spent in a career as a financial advisor I knew was not right for me: I'd pursue many things that were supposed to go along with that professional image. One of these was, I'd always maintained a subscription of the *Wall Street Journal*, which didn't interest me, but I had it lying around as an "image builder." Of course, this is nothing to dwell on and is really no big deal, but it's just to prove that we all do things to some degree that don't match our reality.

Try to truthfully recognize these things, these images, the relationships you thought were necessary to make yourself real, and then recognize that it is not really there at all. In other words, the career you despise is not a true reflection of who you are, but it is a projected image you've made of yourself to make you think you can be happy.

In this exercise, or prayer, or meditation, however it is you decide to make of it, you want to tell yourself that "your salvation can never come from things" you project. You must become aware that what truly saves you and what truly makes you real is already within you and nothing *outside* of you can give you completion.

With this absorbed into your awareness, you can begin to explore along with me, the illusions and the paths which guilt tries to pave for us as constructed by the ego-based mind. In this knowledge, within an instant you will be able to release to the Holy Spirit for reversal or undoing. In this *holy instant* you will have created a *real path* that leads to attaining your true free will, and while seeing what *you don't want*, illusion, fading away.

So in this sense and as a refreshing reminder, ask yourself what is a *holy instant*? It's the time it takes to begin seeing what you do not want in your life begin fading away, while at the same time what you do want is ushered in.

Part III

Reality Is No Fantasy, It's Better

Chapter 27

Where Wholeness Is Joined

In my adolescence during the 1960s going to church was just about an everyday occurrence in the Catholic school system. There was Sunday mass with my parents and daily mass as a start to the school day. I'll admit, I value that education today. But even at that young age I felt something was missing.

The thought of Heaven frightened me more so than hell, only because I never truly believed the fiery realm below was my destination, regardless of their warnings. I certainly didn't want to be wrongfully convicted either, and that is partly why I made sure not to miss mass, while, as well, stay a regular at the confessional booth.

I pictured Heaven as a place of perpetual church services, mandatory with no escaping it. It bothered me that I might not be able to do things in Heaven I truly enjoyed, like sports. It was never suggested Jesus might be seen tossing the football around, although I did envision him as a quarterback rather that a coach. But the Bible does say something about "see how the children play."

I'd picture God on a throne assisted by His cohorts of angels and saints who'd always be on the lookout for those tempted to skip mass. A Catholic Heaven, of course. The thought of getting kicked out of Heaven once there, was a concern I had. These kinds of childish thoughts gave me worrisome notions.

I'd visualize a traditional Heaven with everyone singing to organ hymn music and walking around with hands folded together telling one another "God be with you." These images in my mind at times brought forward a concerned rebelliousness that helped me to anticipate there must be more.

The holy instant is that place where there is more than what your separateness dreams about. It's that timeless naturalness where we express our existence by extending it, but it's not a replacement for learning. If you can realize the Holy Spirit being programmed into your mind as your Teacher as well as your Healer, and remaining so until the holy instant has extended itself for beyond time, you will come to know your true free will as your only desire. Your mind will have then briefly seen yourself clearly and brightly as the whole Son of God, before disappearing into God Himself.

The Holy Spirit has already arranged the necessary events, situations, and people to arrive into your life. Some of these experiences may be seen as good or bad depending on the hold the ego-based mind has on you at that particular time, but where all is essentially in order so that you will eventually carry out your true free will, through His guidance. He will use everything and anything to get your attention while your free will waits for you in time.

What do I mean by "waits for you in time?"

The Holy Spirit will use every ounce of your willingness to guide you, once He sees your readiness level is right, to the intended path where all His efforts are automatic when you offer the truth. His watchfulness over you is limitless in strength and clarity, and he is fully aware of your fears especially where forgiveness is concerned.

* * *

While we are here the Holy Spirit is our Divine Power and is teaching us that forgiveness is release and surely not a concern over loss. Ever since the separation we've learned to feel that when we forgive we're moving into scarcity by giving up something. Adam and Eve lacked dignity in their nakedness while losing paradise—the biggest loss humankind has ever experienced. The thought itself of lack is a scarcity-driven state of mind.

We believe that we lose something, a bit of dignity, when we forgive, and thereby think we deserve some form of compensation or restitution for our generosity.

However, in the real world beyond that tiny speck of separateness, forgiveness is effortless because it's an act of wholeness reflected into the separated world. It entails no loss whatsoever, and, in fact, is what saves us. What does it save us from? you may ask.

Forgiveness is of the separated mind but the thought inspiring it is a reflection of wholeness, which urges the ego-dominated self to look beyond all illusion by overlooking the ego-based mind and finding out what you see. That result is your salvation.

Consider on a dark night in your backyard with hints of the moon glowing, you may see a strange shadow that startles you, an unfamiliar image you think might be a burglar in the night. But when you turn on the porch light you notice the image was only a shadow figure of a tree branch in the wind. It was an illusion after all, and in an instant the light saved you.

When you can see yourself beyond the ego's separateness, you are doing so with real vision by leaving judgment behind, and realizing that Wholeness has no separate parts. You'll also realize at that point there is nothing to forgive, because what is not separate of mind ever needs forgiveness. You can't look beyond wholeness because it is infinite. This real thought of wholeness becomes your release from scarcity thinking and guilt, too.

Listen quietly now to the Holy Spirit as He rushes healing thoughts of abundance into your mind. Healing makes whole because it rids separation. Ask yourself, what really is it that gives you attackful types of thoughts, and do these thoughts make you bright, joyful, and alive? No, they don't, and healing is needed. Rather than dissecting this question with the knife of blame and making more separated thoughts of attack, your willingness to truthfully answer this comes from your Divine Power. Our real *Self* is one with the joy we all want. It can't be wished for, but it is *wanted*, and this in itself is enough to teach you that you have no real need for the special relationship.

We search in these relationships for what we wish to make up for or recover what we've lost or thrown away. By making these special relationships we will never find the value of oneness we are casting aside, but we still yearn for it with all our heart. However, we can join together in experiencing the holy instant as all there is.

How do we achieve this?

By effortlessly accepting others for *wholly* who they are, instead of placing effort into making parts of them into what you wish them to be.

* * *

Each one of us as the whole Son of God or as an integral aspect of the Sonship has such a great need to be inner connected to the willingness of everyone else that its power is astonishing. In that instant of *wanting* is where we are joined in wholeness. This is the definition of love. There can be no other meaning. It causes the free will in each of us to be shared in a purpose that all of us love freely the pursuit of happiness. Love is wholeness of mind. Consider with this effortless integration of true free wills everywhere, which is *cause* having the *effect* of us never being alone.

Let's consider this a lesson by the Holy Spirit whole-mindedly given through me and on to you by way of an ego-based world, that will enable you to automatically relate to what will never leave you, and, too, what you can never leave.

With this understood, how can you be lonely unless God is lonely? Of course, God is certainly not alone with each of us as His "cohorts" sharing the same mind, even with some of us still asleep. Therefore, let's not turn away from the awareness of being complete, likewise, not having to search for completeness, because it will naturally occur.

In order to experience this naturalness, you must not fear surrendering yourself to the love of all there ever could be. It's called *Truth.* Ask yourself, what is the worst that can happen when you make a decision entirely on the truth? Then accept any sense of failure as nothing more than a mistake or a simple error that the Holy Spirit may or may not use later to keep you on the path of your will.

Let's further remember, you do house God within you and as His host you cannot ultimately fail. Your true free will is His Will, and eternally this is a relationship within holiness, and this holiness is all that exists. Feel free to use the following comfortable fact that I have used in my seemingly down times: *Wherever you are at your time of need help will seek you out and find you there.*

When I was writing the rough draft of this book, it was a time where I was waiting all too anxiously to be released early from prison on a signature of the "example-setter" judge that dished me out a ten-year sentence. Due to foreclosures, bank garnishments, and a whole slew of financial reckoning, I had no place to go upon my release. That was until my friend, Ron, of thirty years along with a few family members asked me to not stress but to merely oblige to their assistance.

The universe that you hold within you must be beyond all of the separateness of space, form, and all the illusion we perceive and then project images of. These minds of a joining oneness from beyond the dream of separation are not of bodies at all, but one of the unseparated essence that bonds us, which is Christ, our relationship with one another like rays of sun to the sun.

The relationships you seek while here on earth are already alive and real in everyone you encounter as they dream of their own separateness. Their dream is inside of or a part of your dream. In other words, the image of you is projected in their dream, but only through your own dreaming state of mind. They cannot have a dream without your projection of them, which means their own separation doesn't exist without your own illusive tiny speck of mind that sees form as real life. The good news in this understanding means you do not have to make special of anyone you encounter or come to know.

Of course there are those we meet where we draw to them immediately, more closely than we do to others. Regardless of the closeness involved, there is no need to make a single special thought of it, such as increasing or decreasing what we wish to make special of another individual.

Being a projection of the ego-based mind, special can never be special enough. Something seems to always lack. By seeing that individual for who they truly are—the Christ in them, your brother/sister—only then will we be able to enjoy the relationship for what the Holy Spirit has intended it to be in *your dream of separation* and not theirs. This is where all true relationships exist, and where forgiveness is unreal but is a reflection of your wholeness turned into a projection. What I mean is the reflective thought is manifested into the form you call forgiveness.

Is there truth to actress Ali McGraw's famous line in the movie *Love Story*, when she intimately said to Ryan O'Neal, "Love means never having to say you're sorry." Think about that by having some fun with it. See where it takes your thoughts.

* * *

There's no doubt that the image of the body does have much to do with initiating a relationship. But by allowing truth to take hold you take the body out of the picture that formed where specialness fades away and is nonexistent. You will begin to know when you see the face of Christ in your partner as well as recognizing the dealings of the ego-based mind.

This vision will be the same or similar with others you meet, and some will evolve into something meaningful and progress further while others will be of lesser involvement. Regardless of the depth of these relationships they will all be purposeful where the Holy Spirit is concerned.

To achieve this awareness, it must be natural and cannot be consciously forced. This can be so by keeping your vision away from what you do not understand about another and by focusing on what you do understand, of which gives you joy. You were not brought into this world and brought together to try to understand every little thing about each other. This is not the Holy Spirit's intention, nor should it be yours.

A problem may arise that upsets you in a close relationship, say, with your spouse or significant other. You can choose to remove your concentration from what displeases you, stopping the projection, and rather choose to focus on what makes you happy about him or her—the reflection of unity. You can do this by saying to yourself, "I get so disgusted when she acts this way, but there are so many qualities I love about her."

Once you've accepted this stance on the matter, release your negativity—your wrong-minded notions and thoughts to the Holy Spirit—and be done with it. You'll immediately feel better because wholeness will be reflecting.

Now let's move on and see why this special love relationship can cost you dearly.

Chapter 28

Neutral Thoughts Don't Exist

The special love relationship is a costly illusion primarily because it's hard on you. This emotional roller-coaster ride confuses you over truth and falsity, and the hills and valleys of real and unreal.

When you're young you haven't thought much of the fact, yet. You see every love as the real one that will never end. But once you've matured, after having experienced a few such loves, those peaks and valleys, you can never forget the truth. But unfortunately, that doesn't make the break-ups any easier, because if your heart breaks, it's the huge, irrational, wild, and primitive heart of the child inside you that breaks. You will heal with a lesson learned. Believe me, I used to think "every time I break up, I break down and lose control of myself." This would set me up for being careful "the next time."

But should you really be careful, or is there a better way?

The romantic love is called the special love relationship and actually prevents real love. This is the most telling and worst revealing of all to anyone who wants real love. Romantic love not only won't give it to you, it will actually keep the real thing away. Why? Because when you crave intensity, you cannot even see the people you really need. Real love can only be attained when it's in alignment with your true free will.

The individuals you really need can't see you either because they're in a different world and not interested in people who only remain at the level of the brain, where all emotion is spent. You're shopping for different things. You wish to be swept away in ecstasy, and they want to unite with and be mutually real.

The specialness expected in romance also drives away the comfort real love offers. Even when we have romantic love, we're always on the alert to keep from losing it. We believe we must work hard to sustain whatever brought us the love in the first place, such as our looks, our goodness, our generosity, and sometimes our firmness. We become overly sensitive to any change in our lover's feelings toward us, and we can't seem to find neutrality.

Liking someone is essential of real love, but it's not possible to like anyone you're madly in love with in the special relationship. If you don't believe me, think about this: would you have stayed in a relationship if there were no passion whatsoever? Or, which would you choose if you could choose only one of the following? A sunny, rosy life of bliss and wealth with or without someone to love. Or, an intense love with on-and-off sunshine and cloudy times. If you've felt even a twinge of conflict, you've got problems. You do not want to know the real world; rather, you wish to lose your*self*.

* * *

It's necessary that you accomplish a *shift*, from seeing with your body's eyes over to real vision. With no magic involved, the holy instant is what gets you there. The ego limits your perception of others by seeing only a body, where the Holy Spirit releases your natural vision to awareness of the rays of light representing your holiness with the rays of holiness to all you encounter. This unlimited holiness reaches to God. So what is it that must occur for this shift to become permanent?

We discussed this before in the sense of forgiveness. The shift easily takes place, naturally, within your willingness to forgive, which is the looking beyond ego-based mania. It's in the sensation you gain that shows you more than just a body, with a perception translated by the Holy Spirit that shifts to knowledge. This knowledge is the part of God that represents the Atonement. It's that *something* in you that tells you there's more to your existence than only a body, as well as others you encounter.

The whole mind does not conform to oneness without the naturalness of knowledge. It is the only step waiting for you that God understands because it's all there is. God will not delay in giving you this shift as He releases your vision through the Holy Spirit, once you are ready. To be ready is to be willing but with trust and faith in Him. He is ready for you, but you have not been.

Your willingness must first take you on a journey to look at all the interferences you made in your life, but to see them as illusion. You need to truly understand that they mean nothing. These separated thoughts, or wrong-mindedness, only interfere with your real vision. Everything you see is the result of your thoughts, and you must let go of the belief that these thoughts have no effect. There is no exception.

You see, either you think right-mindedly or wrong-mindedly, truthfully or falsely, real or unreal, with no happy medium. Those that are false and of the unreal wrong-mind make a likeness by using a projected image based on fear and guilt as its foundation. But those thoughts that are true and of the real right-mind create an extended likeness of God. But also remember, however, that a right-minded thought may sometimes be slightly off track due to ego-based influence, but the truth in its willingness is used by the Holy Spirit to set your real vision.

In this vision is where you'll experience pure joy. Have you ever felt you were in a solid direction and if something were to slightly go wrong you knew it could be easily corrected? That's it! This is the right-minded real vision that still may feel some ego tugging, that I'm talking about. With right-mindedness as your strong suit, the ego folds.

* * *

You are learning that the body is the symbol of the ego-based mind, and it strives to constantly make separated thoughts. Each thought separate from the extension of God is an attempt to limit communication, making real vision impossible. Real communication must be unlimited in order to have meaning, and being deprived of real meaning in your life makes completeness tough to experience.

Your incompleteness becomes a continued lacking in all that you pursue, even in your relationships. Real meaning is the only means you have for creating real relationships with no limits. Your thoughts are going to either extend the truth or multiply illusion. You can indeed multiply nothing and will always get nothing. But just as well you cannot extend nothing.

Thoughts are never idle and bring about either peace or war, love or fear. A neutral thought is impossible; thereby a neutral thought can never truly occur. How often do we dismiss fearful thoughts as unimportant, trivial, and not worth bothering over? Never. But we do dwell on them.

It's essential that we recognize them all as equally destructive and equally unreal, because they're not of God. If the word "God," here, in the context of our discussion is too religious sounding for you due to the ego's hold on you, then substitute the word for "Oneness." For me, the word itself, *God*, is easy to understand now, and is comfortable in my usage, but you are not limited to using it. It's important we keep this clear as we move along.

If you try to be complete with the idea that you have no neutral thoughts, but do not actively seek to overlook any "little" thoughts that may tend to elude you, you'll still find it difficult not to make unreal assumptions. Every thought that occurs to you regardless of size or quality that you assign to it is a suitable subject for you to go ahead and tell yourself it cannot be neutral. Then proceed to assign it a label as true or false, real or unreal. Then let go of what is *not* real.

What you can do now is try to get in the habit of accepting any annoying or fearful or attackful-type thoughts, as either of God or of the ego-based mind. You must decide what type of thought it is, because only *you* could ever know. In that instant of decision, that very instant where you lean toward your choice, you have shifted from perception over to knowledge.

Once you have a habit in doing so, you will have established real vision in yourself where neutrality will never be a part of your life. What possibilities for you are there from here?

* * *

In the scenario I used about what you may dislike in your spouse or significant other, you may want to incorporate into your thinking an idea to help the shift. Now that you're learning to naturally shift into real thinking, talk to yourself by saying something like this: *This thought I'm having about her annoying action is not neutral, because neutral thoughts are impossible. If it's not neutral, then what is it?*

You will want this thought to sink in, and then say: *Even though the thought is not neutral, I'm aware it was made by my ego-based mind.* Then, release it to the Holy Spirit for undoing and move on. You must begin to accept responsibility for all your thoughts as either real or unreal.

When you truly feel it is *decision time*, simply ask yourself: *Are these thoughts I'm having about her of God or are they of my ego-based mind?* Then answer quickly without dwelling on the matter, because any dwelling is an opportunity for the ego to trap you into indecisiveness with more thought.

Trust that your newly found knowledge on the matter will enable you to answer that question honestly, in an instant, and without hesitation, and you can move forward in confidence. It can be as easy as this: "Uh-oh, I caught myself making an ego-based thought about her comment that triggered a judgmental thought. It's not real, and I'm done with it."

It really is that simple. Make your decision within yourself quickly without feeling arrogant. If you're totally truthful, arrogance is only seen by ego eyes.

Chapter 29

Attraction beyond the Body

We've been learning that in the holy instant your awareness is away from the body. Beyond the body is where you extend in the likeness of God. The relationships you have that are real will always be reflected without limits, like rays of sunshine are to the sun. But in order to share this vision of likeness—the extension of Oneness—you must surrender the ego-mind's use for the body as your primary means for living a life of purpose. You must accept the fact that the ego-based mind has no purpose you'd want to share with it.

Once you've made this decision the body will then have no choice but to follow along for the joy ride and be loyal to your real Self. Allow the body to follow your lead into reality and away from illusion. You'll find that leaving the ego behind will bring forward in your mind pure joy where truth is never questioned.

With the ego wishing to limit everyone you encounter to a body for its own purposes related to fear, and when you are sold on its self-made purposes, is when you choose to use its methods for operation—its separated thought system—to turn purpose into achievements. You'll never totally reach your goal because there will always be the wish for more. Since the ego is unreal, it can never have a real purpose and is why you cannot be complete as long as you follow its guidance. Any false strength in the goal is wasted energy.

No one can successfully divide their strength between the real and the unreal, or, let's say, between Heaven and Hell, and for that fact, God or the ego. There is no neutral zone within the Oneness of all that exists, true Creation. When you release your power of the Creation to the Holy Spirit, your real purpose will be given you. Actually, you will have uncovered it from its hiding place.

* * *

The ego-based mind demands limits so it may make littleness on ineffectual things it thinks is important, and operates like this because it lacks the power of true *cause*. This oneness of *cause and effect* is creativity, and the ego has none because it has no *cause*. Its nearest potential is projecting images of what it wishes were so.

When we limit our sight of another individual to a body, which is what you do unless you release an individual from it, you are denying that individual's messages to you directed by the Holy Spirit.

Whatever the message intended for you through another's body cannot be perceived with these limits you've placed on that individual. Here, you have limited yourself. How do you release someone from his body? By surrendering your own projected image of another individual to the Holy Spirit for the necessary undoing, which is a reversal of the projection, so that He may or may not directly use it for a purpose according to the plan of Creation—the plan set for you.

The minds of you and your brothers/sisters everywhere are already continuously in sync with one another, and you don't need to force or manipulate anything. All you need to do is accept this union yourself, whether they realize it or not. Most often their physical existence won't realize your vision, but likewise you may not realize theirs. In this sense you're never alone. So allow the Holy Spirit to open your vision to Oneness (God), which is experienced in the love of Truth, and you will naturally become aware of the need for your creations as they reflect into the minds of humankind.

You will begin having a joyful vision of the simple eternal, because you'll have its simple knowledge. You'll have no need of ego manipulation. No one can experience this and linger in a special relationship, but they will have joyfully understood the purpose of that relationship without limits of any kind. Wouldn't you likely learn from the limiting and then exchange it for the limitless?

If so, why do so many of us still search for the special and remain limited to a body? Once you've learned the lesson of having limits imposed by the ego-based mind, then you'll certainly have the knowledge of choosing the limitless that gives you real freedom.

* * *

Many of us really have no idea of the limits we've placed on our perceptions, and no idea of the reality that waits us. Let's try to remember that our attraction to guilt opposes our attraction to God.

God's attraction is always unlimited, but because of the power we have which is of Him and just as great as His, we are able to choose *not* to throw out love by *not* giving this power to the ego. This is wasting it, because whatever we invest in guilt, likewise in that same ratio we take away from the power of God. Not that He will ever run low or lack power, but you will only delay the accomplishment of full Atonement. In this delay we must deal with continued illusion.

When this happens, your sight grows weak and dim and limited; you become more irritable and unsettled, living in fear and lacking confidence in yourself; faith and trust are hard to come by, all because you've tried to separate the Father in you from the Son in you.

By doing so you try to split apart oneness, and this limits real communication. This is why you pray to God as though He is far away outside of you when you ask that "He hears your request." You begin to experience the falsity of lack because your integral part in the Sonship is lacking. This is why the Atonement process—your awakening—then lacks due to your separated

153

thoughts that only further imprison you. You get stuck in a mode of "needing more."

When the body no longer attracts you as something of value by using it for gain, you will have cut off all ego-based interference in communication, keeping your thoughts as free as God's. Then you can begin to allow the Holy Spirit to teach and guide you to use the body for purposes of communication and choose to let go of its use for separation and attack. You will learn that you have no need for a body at all, *but* the Holy Spirit does need your body for now, in time, a device to bring you back *Home*. By bringing you back *Home* all of God's Creation come with you, and this is why your true free will must ultimately be accomplished, with nothing to fear.

Think about it. While experiencing a holy instant did you have any concerns at all about the body? Likewise, did you force the body to get you there? Your only experience in that holy instant was the attraction of Oneness (God).

When you can accept this attraction as undivided, meaning no separate parts whatsoever, but, rather, completely whole, then you will have joined Him. Isn't it natural for any one of us to make our Father proud? And He is proud, but He wants us to know that in reality we've been joined all along, and in an instant the reality of this relationship becomes all you could ever want, because it's whole. In reality, there is nothing else.

Chapter 30

Her Distant Engine of Fate

You may doubt the Holy Spirit will do His part because you feel you're running out of time. Or, you may think that time is running out on you.

If time seems to be getting in your way you will know this to be the ego's own striving to make things happen. But just hang on, because by your own willingness, which is not about striving, you will be instructed what to do and in a timely order, that is, of course, if it is your intended purpose.

Let me share the story with you about fellow author Irene Kampen. Irene is best known for *Life without George*, a warm and funny book on which the Lucille Ball television show was based. She has written several other books, all of them characterized by the same wry humor, all drawn from her experiences as a middle-class suburban woman trying to hold her own in a confusing and not always friendly world.

Irene Kampen has a loyal following of readers. Her books and the TV show have made her fairly wealthy. She has done a good deal of reflecting about her fame, as it came to her suddenly and unexpectedly in her middle age. Before it came, she was stuck in a dark cloud cover where light was severely obscured.

"If somebody had come up to me back in 1960 and predicted I was going to write books," she said, "I would have thought 'how ridiculous.' I had no idea of writing any book. And if that person would have predicted I'd be a successful author, I would have laughed." She added, "I was utterly miserable. There was nowhere to turn, and my life seemed to be over."

But then a miracle started taking place. Circumstances of which she knew was not luck. "This was too good and strong to be considered luck," she told one interviewer. When the cloud cover cleared for Irene, the entire course of her life was drastically changed.

Irene Kampen knows it was all planned from the beginning by God, no perception of luck about it. "I was put on earth to make people laugh," she has said. "Everything that has happened to me, including all that misery and suffering, was designed to get my attention and bring this about. I am where I am today because of Divine arrangements," she said.

She went on to say in many ways, how, in order for that drastic change to have happened in her life, hundreds of different types of events had to take place with just the right people in just the right ways at just the right times. All of the events had to fit together like pieces of a puzzle. If one piece had been missing, the whole thing would have collapsed, the process would have stopped, and today she might still be stuck where she was in 1960.

* * *

I certainly can relate with Irene when she talked about feeling that her life was engineered from the very beginning, so that when she did become a writer of books, she would be equipped with a load of experiences to write about. Not to mention her character so shaped by events that the writing would help folks feel good.

Irene enjoyed her college days at the University of Wisconsin where she met the man who would soon become her husband. The Second World War was raging at the time, and she married the man who went off to war as a bomber pilot. She had a feeling the relationship was not exactly right, as though something was missing, but she temporarily dismissed the idea and went on planning to be a good wife. The bomber pilot, now her husband, returned from the war and he and Irene bought a house in Levittown, at Long Island, New York. A daughter was born.

Times were happy for a while and a few years later her husband ran off with another woman. After two years of separation, Irene was divorced with a small daughter to raise on her own.

This period was the bottom of her life. The only thing she had to live for was her daughter. It was a dark time in the late 1950s when she started going to church, and she admits to going in search of comfort. She had never been seriously interested in religion before, but she was desperate to get any comfort she could. Her only prayer was that she was willing to do whatever it took to get on some kind of a positive path.

Irene didn't know that a distant engine of fate was already beginning a slow start of the ignition turning in her direction. Across the continent out in California, the often-stormy marriage and business partnership of Lucille Ball and Desi Arnez was breaking up. Irene recalls reading about their problems in the tabloids. She felt a brief pang of sympathy for the red-head actress, and then some time passed when Irene had forgotten all about Lucille Ball.

Irene had some writing experience from her college days, and a small job at a small newspaper column didn't last. She ran into an old friend that suggested she ought to gather all the columns she'd saved and put them into book form. Irene said thank you but doubted the wisdom of the advice. She was unaware at the time this was the first of some moves in God's miraculous manipulation of events, as one day she stepped into a local library to return a book a few days earlier than she had originally planned.

* * *

Upon standing at the book return counter, Irene held a book of alleged humor written by a woman where Irene found its content *not* funny at all. In fact, she even said to the librarian, "I would write a funnier book than that."

The librarian that day was in a foul, awful mood. Librarians get tired of hearing so many comments like this, but usually nod politely and keep their thoughts to themselves.

This librarian, however, felt the need to get something off

her chest. She sharply suggested that Irene Kampen put her typewriter where her mouth was. The librarian went off on Irene by adding things like: "It's easy to say you can write a book." That librarian went on to say people come into the library all the time with attitudes that they can write better books than what's on the library shelves.

Irene was stung, but also encouraged by the librarian's fit of rage on that particular day. Gears started to mesh inside her. That night she sat at her typewriter and began a book about the experiences of two divorced women living in a house with two kids. She worked on it excitedly just as I am doing in this instant, now, on this book that is now in your hands. Time has suspended itself in this instant of holiness as I joyfully write and while you read it.

Irene had no idea what she would do with it and didn't know why she was writing it. She just went on writing it without thinking about the next page. She knows now that the urge came from somewhere beyond her physicalness, and I must say her story has inspired me to write with minimal effort from my heart. A great example of the extension of Oneness within the holy instant.

One thing led to another with Irene, and one day on a train she ran into an old friend she hadn't seen in ten years. Her friend was now a TV writer. He asked to borrow the manuscript of the book for a while and would get back to her. This meeting was an essential piece to the puzzle.

He loved it. He showed it to a Twentieth Century Fox TV editor. She thought she liked it but wasn't yet sure. She suggested it be sent to a New York literary agent she knew. The agent loved it, and found a publisher who loved it.

* * *

Out west in California, Lucille Ball and Desi Arnez were grumpily parted by now. The somewhat "soured" actress over men was looking for a new "vehicle," as they say in show business. She and her friend Vivian Vance wanted to find some kind of situation comedy in which there were no prominent roles for men. They had been hunting for about three years and were growing desperate.

One day Lucille Ball's agent picked up a copy of Irene Kampen's book, and that was it. The show ran for seven years and is still appearing in reruns today.

Perhaps your own interpretation of the events of this story differs from mine, in that of how miracles occur. That is fine. However, don't "waste your time" trying to sell your interpretation to anybody else. The only individuals who will listen to you will be those who already know what you know.

Once people have reached conclusions about the nature of miracles, even vague conclusions, they hardly ever change their minds. For you to try and change their minds means you are seeking a special relationship. It doesn't take specialness to gain knowledge and to live a life of purpose.

Chapter 31

Think about It: What Lies beyond a Dark Sky?

It's difficult to see ourselves as the only Son of God—His only Child—let alone understand how wholeness is Creation. Then to call ourselves "Christ" raises even more questioning. There you have it, confusion, and the influence of illusion.

The negativity in our surroundings and our dwelling on them due to our fears seem to dictate our destiny. We're always afraid of repercussions. This is where the illusion of sin is projected by wrong-mindedness. What we believe to be sin is made by the body, because it actually takes place in the dream of separation. Dreams of any kind are not real and so in this sense how can sin be possible? It can't. What is seen as sin is nothing more than being lost in the dream and afraid to know true reality. This makes us doubtful of what is truly real.

Our confusion and doubt over reality was portrayed by the apostle Thomas when he asked Jesus; "If we don't know where you are how can we know the way?" Jesus answered Thomas in saying: "No one comes to the Father except through me," and then said, "If you really knew me, you would know my Father as well." Jesus was telling us that the steps necessary (the way) of the Christ within each of us is what inspires (the truth) us to the reality (the life) of the Divine Guidance given us so that we may live our true free will.

This was evident in the previous true story about Irene Kampen. In her reality she overlooked her errors and had forgiven herself for what led to her misery, and only then could she awaken to a clear, inspired path ahead.

The forgiving we do by looking beyond ego-based behavior is a quick fix to clearing the cloud cover that obscures the light of the real world (reality, truth). Sin exists only in the obscurity of that dark cloud cover, but none of it is real. Beyond the darkness of it all is true reality, past all the non-sense of duality. Remember, we've learned there is no middle ground, so what can possibly be real, true or false, light or darkness? What lies beyond a dark sky?

* * *

What happens in dreams isn't real. As the dreamer of the dream, how could you ever realize the dream is only a dream, and that it is unreal? But sometimes in what's called "lucid dreaming," one can be alert just enough to realize partial awakening and slightly sense the unreality of the dream state. However, it still remains fact the part of the mind doing the dreaming is involved in illusion and doesn't recognize reality.

Only when we awaken from the dream does it become apparent that the dream has had no real effect at all as to who we are and our intended purpose. We wish to believe that fantasy can become reality, so we work at making it the purpose of our lives, which always leads to guilt in some fashion of its many desires and designs. We train our brains to adhere to the fantasy, a wish, a false desire, however you wish to name it, and it is always something we're not.

Was Irene Kampen a part of the dream as she wrote her book that led to the Lucille Ball show? Certainly, and so were the many who laughed with joy in a comfort that felt safe, secure, and at home.

However, it was the reflection of her within her true free will and of those she pleased that was the *Self* that doesn't dream, the whole mind behind the direction of the dream that is unseparated. It had a reflection of true light into the dream manifesting as form. You may choose to see this as confusing or you may choose to reflect on its reality. It's only confusing to the ego-based mind that always chooses to dissect it and then project images of it.

Look at it this way: When I sleep in bed at night and have a great dream about playing a super thirty-six-hole round of golf against my golf buddy, Dirty Mike, and when I know I've beaten him many times before, I also know while I dream such a feat is possible. My point is, a good-size part of my mind knows how much I love the game and sinking putt after putt on Dirty Mike.

If you can get by my bit of humor in this, try to remember, the dream of separation is humankind's tiny, little desire, collectively, to be separate from God's Mind. It's the errant, runaway thought of a "better paradise." That said, now we see why Eve tested the apple.

We were dragged into the dream collectively, but the real part which is the whole mind remains as God's extension being alert to it all and slowly awakens. In this awakening process is where your true free will exists and is the Idea of God. You and I are that Idea.

* * *

Can you in this instant render the ego silent and use your newly found vision to go within yourself and on to see the One Idea of God, which you share with everyone in all walks of life? Certainly you can. That is forgiveness. You are forgiving yourself by letting go of illusion and hanging on to only truth. It's your choice.

You are as He created you, and dreams cannot change that. Your accepting this makes all forms of temptation powerless because it has no meaning. In that instant the ego-based mind is silent for as long as you allow that instant to last. You have let go of the ego, but it only seems to creep back in. Because you are of God you have the power to obliterate the ego.

In your acceptance of Truth as the Being of God and His Creation, within time your reflection of the holy instant will increase in length. In these periods is where you create, just as I am doing now as I write. It is an instant of bliss for me and is certainly holy at that. And, in this same instant you are reading, or should I say, "reflecting," on my words as to how they pertain to you and your life, yes? Time has suspended itself from where I sit now to where you are, in this instant, because we both are reflecting a *wanting* to know more while we're temporarily stuck in the dream of separation.

The sounds of the world become still and quiet and background static doesn't faze you while you are contemplating this, yes? The sights of this world around you are not seen the same as before and sort of fade, no? Then, they disappear, making all the unreal and separated thoughts that the world ever held wiped away forever by this One Idea of your Divinity; do you see it?

Just as Irene Kampen, where her mind was typing away: What is it you hold dear? In that holy instant of thought is your sanity restored because illusion is gone and reality is all there is?

Sure, you may see time ticking away, leaving us with pasts and moving us into futures, but while it's happening you are either reflecting reality or projecting fantasy. Which is it for you? If you are reflecting reality, you will experience what you envision. If you're projecting fantasy, you'll live illusion upon illusion.

You might be thinking this is ridiculous, and for some, too good to be true, and for others, they know exactly what I mean. But all of your accusations are correct, and are either of the ego-based mind, or of the Mind of God. There is no in between.

When I sometimes have difficulty in assumptions like this or have my doubts, I'll always ask myself one question that sets my sights to a sensation I can be comfortable with. That question is, where will I be once my body has died? My answer alone always brings me to my reality and I feel at Home immediately. Here is why, I've discovered, and in its simplicity: *Truth is light and nothing is behind or beyond it, and so it is the real strength of which we all are that is sinless.*

* * *

By accepting that you are as God created you, which is eternal, you have reached or uncovered the Son of God by using the Christ Mind, which you are. You have encountered your true *self,* which is whole and complete. It's the same Oneness that created Irene Kampen's willingness to pursue her true free will, which can only be the extension of her own but shared naturalness that resulted in a writing career. It is the *Self* that directed her into that library on that given day to greet the sarcastic but inspiring librarian.

It's that same *Self* she shared with the librarian, the TV writer, the literary agent, the publisher, and the number of others whose events in their own lives helped to shape the accomplishments of this one individual's free will, which led to her purpose so that she could light up the lives of others, including Lucille Ball, that in turn pleased many audiences with her television show.

Was all of this that happened with Irene a part of the dream of life, form, time, space, and separation? It most certainly was. But Irene's reality from behind all form, directed and carried out this portrayal of love, rather than the ego-based mind controlling it for further projection resulting in further separation of Oneness. This was Irene's participation in the Atonement, the undoing of separation.

We could go on and on and then some more, but I feel you're shifting from physical vision to real vision, and you're realizing this in your mind which is of a Source we both share. Your alertness to all of this causes a slow shift in the awakening of the rest of the world. A position is changed, and this is the process of Atonement.

All that is required of you to see this more clearly is to continuously take your real vision—your reflections of reality beyond the body—and lay all self-made images aside. Take yourself beyond the body and beyond the list of projected attributes you've made for yourself and listen to the absolute truth that is your inner voice. Trust it, because it is you.

Chapter 32

Are You Substituting Fantasy as an Idea of Truth?

A good question as the title of this chapter asks that you give an honest answer, only to yourself; it need not be shared with anyone. I hope you're beginning to understand that it is in our fantasies where the wish to change reality lies, and we can add, it's in trying to change what we are.

This is fearful because by the wish itself we believe we have changed reality. There is such an emphasis on pushing ourselves beyond our own naturalness, and we understand this as being our power. Guilt sets in, and deep down inside we know this power to be unreal, where we begin making excuses when it doesn't prevail. We could say "self-made reasoning."

We cannot truly be faithful to two teachers who guide us in opposite directions. What we use for fantasy, we deny for truth. But on the other hand, what you give of yourself to truth is kept from fantasy and allows your real and natural self to be extended. There's nothing special in this because it's the Oneness of Truth. Specialness requires duality, of two or more, which is the fragmented ego-based mind's thought system that is separate from reality.

When you think that some miracles are more difficult to perform than others, your thoughts are telling you there are some things you would back off from and take away from the truth. I use the word "perform" because miracles are real thought performances, a manifestation that has been reflected from reality.

My point is, we tell ourselves that truth cannot deal with our fantasies, only out of the fear of having to give them up. We like to keep them protected from the truth. Quite simply put, the miracle is the power that heals all pain, and your lack of faith in it, and its power, leaves you hanging on to fantasy. You're simply not realizing what this does to your contribution to the whole Sonship. When you choose fantasy, ever so slightly, that much is denied from truth, and truth is what constitutes wholeness.

Your part in the whole Sonship is where all your real successes in life exist, and, of course, is where your real relationships are built. Jesus discussed this with his friends by using a parable that they could understand or relate to at that period of time. It was about the two men who built their houses. One man built his house on a foundation of rock deep into the earth (wholeness), and the other man built his house quicker, but on sand (fantasy). The house on sand washed away (died); where the house on rock was able to weather all storms (eternally lived).

As long as you make an order of difficulty in miracles you will be judging the healing process, and life will be difficult for you. Your relationships will suffer as a result. You will have established an order of reality by giving some of it to the ego and some of it to the Holy Spirit.

With this middle ground you then learn to deal with part of the truth in one way, and in another way for other parts. But Truth has no separate parts, and what you are doing is substituting fantasy as an idea to fit in as truth. To split truth apart is to destroy it by making it seem to be meaningless. This is what humankind has been doing ever since Eve demanded that Adam also partake in the tree of knowledge.

We can say Adam's firm attack on Eve over her obsession with fantasy was due to his lack of forgiveness. The ego began fragmenting, and "blame" and "excuses" were invented.

* * *

Do you truly think you can bring truth to fantasy and learn truth's meaning through the eyes of illusion? Truth has no perspective at all within a fantasy. Anything of fantasy realizes itself as being unstable, and is always looking for a way out of confusion. By trying to bring truth to a fantasy you're trying to make nothing into something, or make the unreal become real. What the ego makes can never be real and is why it doesn't last.

But on the other hand, to give illusions to the truth is to enable truth to teach that illusions are unreal, and a way to let go of them. In doing so, you must be willing to release all of your confusion to the Holy Spirit.

Here's what you can do:

Be willing to give Him all of your questionable truths and give yourself a bit of time to listen for answers. Your Teacher of Oneness and not of duality will give you the vision you need so you can choose between the real and the unreal, truth or falsity, and love over fear. He will know when you're ready to receive these lessons in an appropriateness that is right for you, based on your readiness level.

You need only to concern yourself with the willingness to uncover the knowledge that is within you and leave perceptions behind as you thank them for their lead. Also remember that when you become disturbed or upset and lose your peace of mind because someone else is trying to solve his problem through fantasy, you are refusing to forgive yourself for the same thing. You are holding both of you away from truth, which is what was denied by both of you.

You simply can never make others have the same vision as you have, but you can welcome their vision as their own. All you can do is allow your true self to be seen for what you are. Either they recognize it as real for them or they do not. It is not up to you to prove their fantasy as unreal.

However, the Holy Spirit may use you and your body as His Teaching aid for lessons of others without you even realizing it. By looking beyond the errors of your brother/sister you are seeing forgiveness in action, and you are being a forgiving individual.

A Course in Miracles states ever so sharply: "What you reserve for yourself, you take away from Him Who would release you. Unless you give it back it is inevitable that your perspective on reality will be warped and uncorrected."

Chapter 33

Who Can Help Me?

While I was in prison my time was heavily consumed with studying, contemplating, and writing about the influences of Light I've come to know. The knowledge is *forgiveness*.

This chapter is based on an article I'd written on forgiving one's self, first, before he or she can forgive others, and this article was well received by a regional newspaper.

At that time I was struggling for a closing idea for the article and was soon rescued from mind boggling. This type of thing had often obsessed me until I'd simply trust, and get a grip on myself as well as my patience. Always when a line or two or so was needed, somehow in some manner my attention would be brought to the words that were waiting for me. Writing has been a tremendous lesson for me—the Light shining on my path.

A story was told to me as a joke about a mountain climber. It was presented nicely and appropriately by a fellow prisoner, while we sat on a bench in the prison yard one sunny morning just after dawn. I'd just finished a brisk walk—a routine that not only helped my sanity behind a double-razor-wire fence, but also kept a healthy blood flow through my body. The endorphins seemed to lend a tranquilizing and painkilling effect that endorsed a positive day ahead.

Also up early that day, I sat next to Ed Nezmith, an inmate friend whom I'd often chatted with about prison life, life in general, and the problems of the world. Sometimes our talks would go on for an hour or so, and we'd seem to inspire each other during dismal times of imprisonment.

Ed is similar to my age, and we met during my fourth year in prison, when he'd already completed his twentieth year of a life sentence.

Coincidentally, both Ed and I are from the same hometown community, which was unusual being that Hocking Prison, one of Ohio's thirty-three prisons, was about a four-hour drive from our Massillon–Canton home area. Normally, prisoners are awarded a facility closer to home to accommodate family visits. But, regardless, our hometown advantage made for some friendly reminiscing, even to include our separate high schools playing each other in the big football rivalry that continues today.

Ed was hanging on by a thread of hope that he may one day be paroled. But due to the strict parole board and its tight guidelines, deep down Ed's spirit knew parole in the near-to-distant future was a gloomy possibility. He had almost no chance. But I did admire the little flicker of light he held for freedom that seemed to keep my own light flaming. Ed refused to put freedom from his mind and was always able to let go of a possibility for disappointment if he'd never be released. Ed told me that forgiveness has given him freedom within prison.

* * *

The conversation that morning mainly was all Ed, and he had plenty to say. I listened with a friendly ear. He was dealing with a life sentence; he was opening up to me about how he longed just to have a definite release date. He was happy for me in that I'd soon be getting my life outside of prison back and putting the past behind me, while becoming a better individual as a result of not only my errors, but also of the experiences thereof.

Speaking with Ed much of the time was inspiring for me, and in prison we all find out quickly that our own individual knowledge comes from the heart, and not from any special degrees or certificates the world awards us with. Ed always had a good joke available at a moment's notice, and always with an encouraging punch line that made one peek at a bit of his wisdom as you laughed with him.

When I asked my good friend to expand more about his feelings and how he was dealing with the fact of being locked up for the rest of his life, he basically volunteered that he'd made the choice some years ago to forgive himself, and that, he said, has made all the difference in being "somewhat" a free man.

Ed said he always held faith that the family of his victim in a murder case may already have forgiven him. He tragically shot and killed his wife of twenty-three years as a result of his addiction to heroin. The substance abuse began with prescription opiates for a back problem from several bullets he took while in the Vietnam War. The doctor gradually withdrew Ed from the opiates, but one thing led to another and he was in search of more pain relief, and soon found himself on heroin. He was hooked. I'll add, it is so surprising the number of murder cases I've seen in prison due to substance abuse, and heroin seems to be top of the list.

Ed has accepted the fact that his in-laws may never forgive him. He and his wife had one child who died just after Ed entered prison, a suicide.

He also accepts that what happened was out of his control because heroin controlled him. It's no cop-out, because he also realizes that the drug addiction could have been treated. Ed has made sure a few years ago that his in-laws know of his remorse and regret, and says now he leaves it in God's hands. Ed has never heard back from them.

He has learned to "let go," he says, of all that went down on that rainy and dark night when two gunshots rang through his house, and still ring in his head, "somewhat." Ed now lives his time out in this world with an understanding of his own forgiveness, what it means, regardless of where he must physically live. He says he feels that being in prison has nothing to do with why he chose to forgive himself. He added, forgiving himself was really a small step he took, but is a great accomplishment in his understanding of God. Ed has finally come to know himself.

With the trust Ed had in me, he went on to tell me his entire story over the many occasions the two of us would walk or sit in the yard. Ed doesn't deny his guilt of the murder, but no longer allows the guilt to control him.

The humorous story he has told me about the *mountain climber* has been a gift to me, and I think of Ed each time I tell this story. I will admit I had to alter a few words here and there from how it was originally told to me, you know, clean up the prison verbiage, so it could be appropriate for this book. But its point remains unchanged.

As I already mentioned, the timing of receiving this gift from Ed couldn't have come at a better time. It inspired me to complete the article that went on to be what I consider a success. You see, I am positive it has helped many in a time of need while my article was passed along to addiction centers and Alcoholic Anonymous meetings. Here it is: It's called, "Who Can Help Me?"

* * *

A mountain climber strives carefully, being well trained and in excellent physical shape, to be the first to make it to the top of the steep rocky mountain in record-breaking time.

As he pushes and pulls his way upward to within three-quarters of his destination—the top—he makes a slight error and loses his footing. A rock slips out from under him, his safety harness breaks, and his body tumbles downward, banging and scraping and sliding down alongside the steep slope. Surely he is doomed and most definitely out of the competition.

Suddenly out of nowhere he is able to grab on to a small tree trunk that seems to have grown sideways out of the slope. He can only hang on with one arm as his other arm seems to be broken from the fall. As he looks below him with his legs and feet dangling, all he can see is at least a thousand feet below of rushing, rocky, white-water rapids. He quickly ponders his fate, realizing the fall alone would surely bring him to death. He is without choices and is upset at the one error he made that caused him to lose footing, a situation he feels he can't escape. He realizes he tried to reach too far too quickly.

He peers up to the clear blue sky with the sun's rays blurring his eyesight, and he asks God to help him. "Oh, Lord my God, please tell me what to do now in my time of need." He cries again, this time more anxiously, "I've been a good individual all my life, hardly ever missed church on Sunday mornings, please don't fail me now."

God answers him by gently saying, "My son, I am here to help you, just as I have always been with you before. Listen carefully, my son, and do as I instruct you. I will guide you through this."

The climber takes a nervous gasp for air and says a quick prayer. "Thank you, God, for coming to my rescue. Go ahead, please, tell me, I will do whatever you say! But hurry, I don't believe I can hang on much longer!"

God shouts out from the clear blue sky in a demanding demeanor. "My son, let go of the tree right now. You will be fine, and in fact, you'll be better than ever, but you must let go now, in this instant."

This was far too much for the climber to handle, and as he hangs on he screams out to God in fear and rage. "Please, God, you must not understand, if I let go I'll surely fall into the rocky rapids below and I'll die. I ask you, is this truly what you want me to do?"

This time God bellows out from above and His Voice shakes the whole mountain and echoes throughout the canyon. "My Son, I'm telling you as your Father who loves you and knows you well, you must let go now and do not think otherwise. Forget about your mistake and let go of that tree now. Do as I ask!"

The climber, in tears, looks up at the clear sky and then looks below in fear. Anxiously he glares upward, again, with tears pouring and asks God one final question: "God, I've always had faith in you," he mutters, "but I must ask, is there anyone else up there that can help me?"

* * *

I hope this story raised a smile, or a smirk, or a nice chuckle, which is its intention. But isn't this exactly what we do in our lives? Are not our ego-based separated thoughts turned into our decision making, leaving Divine Guidance aloof?

We've discussed the Oneness of mind each of us consists of, and within this Oneness is the Self we call Christ. Although we are one Self as the whole Christ, we seem to experience ourselves as two, being forgiving and unforgiving, loving and hating, mind and body. It is as though we need this duality to survive.

This split into opposites brings on conflict and leads us to forming a perception of why we think we are based on the mix of feelings. We try to perfect these opposites within us into a solution that works. These opposites can never be compatible. The real solution to this error in thought is to understand that truth and illusion can never mix. Let's move on and learn what will mix.

Chapter 34

Restoring Christ in You

It is an absolute and certain fact of the universe that Truth and illusion cannot unite, nor become compatible. No matter how diligent we try or whatever means we use, oneness cannot be formed out of these two opposites.

Until we've accepted this, we will attempt an endless list of goals we can't reach. We'll continue to have a senseless series of wasting time and effort, hopefulness and doubt, each being useless as ever and failing just like the next ones to come along.

Problems that begin with no meaning will always have no meaning and cannot be resolved within yourself and these problems are the means for constant conflict and can never be resolved, and good and evil, forgiving and unforgiving can have no meeting place. The self you made, your ego, can only project images and will never reflect the face of Christ, which you're learning now is your true Self.

Likewise, your true *Self* cannot be split in two and still be what *it* is and will forever be. Your mind and body cannot both exist separately, so make no attempt at reconciling the two, because one simply denies that the other can be real.

If all that you are about is of a physical nature, then your mind is gone from your self-concept because it has no place in which it can call itself *you*. If you are spirit, then the body must be meaningless to your reality.

The Atonement process is where spirit uses the mind as a means to find its *Self*-expression, and the mind that serves the spirit is at peace and filled with joy. The power of the mind comes from spirit as it happily fulfills its function, here, in the midst of time and space and form. Yet the mind can also see itself divorced from spirit, and perceive itself captured within a body, which it confuses with itself. Without its function, then, it has no peace, and happiness is alien to its thoughts. It then believes it is owned by the body which rules over a destiny that is delusional.

* * *

I'd like to share an example for our discussion here, about my family's inheritance. A certain chosen few of us in my large family, to include myself, and thanks to my mother, have inherited a hairline cowlick. This spectacle has proven to be stubborn to the women in the family who own it, with their hairstyling efforts.

My oldest daughter, Erin, when she was a pre-teenager would look in the mirror with frustration at the *problem-causing cowlick.* She was realizing a life ahead of herself being teased and annoyed by this cowlick that would not part, in more ways than just leaving.

Being the caring grandmother who my mother has always been for my daughters, she quickly and sensibly convinced Erin that her hairline problem should not be seen as a problem at all. In fact, Erin's grandma proved to her it could be seen as a unique quality that enhanced her beauty. Something the other girls at school would never be able to sport.

My mom taught my daughter how to manage the cowlick rather than the cowlick managing Erin. A few years later, Erin was willing to pass along this same lesson to my second daughter, Megan, who had the same identical enhancement. Erin and Megan today are both considered by men in general to be extremely elegant women with lovely hairstyles. We can say they both brought their spirit to their minds to project an image of beautiful hair, as a reflection of the beauty of their reality.

Yet mind apart from spirit cannot have real thoughts. That's separation. It will have denied its Source, choosing to be separate, and the result is seeing oneself as helpless, limited, and weak.

175

In this weakness you become totally disassociated from your function, and feel alone. Your mind feels everything everywhere is massed against itself, and the mind hides away in a weak body. This is when you feel you must bring together a happy median between *like and dislike*. But there is no reality in a median.

But let's not waste more time on this. Who can resolve a senseless conflict of a dream? Even if there were to be a median as a resolution, what could it really mean in the truth of what it is? What purpose could it serve, other than for you to let go of it and side with the truth?

* * *

Your mind and spirit are personalized. What do I mean by this?

Any and all salvation you seek cannot make illusions real, nor solve a problem that doesn't truly exist. Perhaps you hope it can so you can think you have problems which you really do not have. Sound familiar? Yet, would you desire God's plan for your true free will to bring you pain and fail to give you freedom?

Your true *Self*, the Christ in you, retains *its* thoughts and they remain within your mind and in the Mind of God. The Holy Spirit is what saves you in mind boggling, and directs you to your free will through peace of mind, without any conflict. Salvation is whatever manner you deem as being saved, and is merely a thought you share with God, because His Mind is your mind.

With your mind inside of God's Mind, salvation is kept among the thoughts your *Self* holds dear for you. How often, even if briefly, like an instant, have you felt secure in your thoughts about plans you have? That is it! Even if it's only an instant it is your true *self* clearing the path ahead. What is the difference between the *Self* and the Holy Spirit? you ask. No difference, because there is no median. You are *it*. Your true *self* is Christ, mind and spirit personalized. This is why we're calling the trueness about you, the *Face of Christ*.

If you feel you've lost this personalized thought, you can find it where the presence of your Oneness is guaranteed. Remember, the Holy Spirit of God is the director of your mind. He is easy to find as He holds onto the truth about everything.

Therefore, your honesty with yourself about everything is the Holy Spirit leading the way for you. For example, I truthfully asked both my daughters, Erin and Megan, now as adults, a simple question. I asked, "Girls, was the cowlick truly bothering the real *you*, or did it bother your ego-based mind?"

* * *

Your salvation comes from the *Self* through the Holy Spirit who acts as the bridge connecting your perceptions to real knowledge. The "Great Communicator," we can say. He makes it possible for you to know Christ. So listen, patiently, to the Voice inside your vision. What's it telling you? What are you capable of?

Look within and recognize salvation coming from Christ. Salvation is the process of living in the light of your true free will. You must seek these thoughts and claim them real and as your own, regardless of what the world tells you. These are your own real thoughts you have been denying, thoughts that have allowed your mind to go on wandering aimlessly in a world of fantasy. Your real thoughts are what save you, regardless of how the ego has been phrasing the coin.

Once you feel saved and in the direction of your free will, Christ will welcome it and give it peace. By feeling true strength, your thoughts about your free will are going to flow or extend from your spirit to the spirit in all things created by this Oneness. Confusion will be gone, and you will be restored to your true Self—the Christ in you.

Christ knows you cannot fail. Perhaps your mind remains a bit uncertain. But don't be too concerned, the ego is jealous and is afraid of what you know. The joy you experience will be enough to draw darkness to your light. Believe me when I say, often, and even at this moment in this instant as I write these words, I hear my ego telling me no one will wish to read this book. But I've learned to quickly turn it over to the Holy Spirit, and simply move on.

Each time you suggest to your frantic mind that your free will comes from Christ, you walk a clearer, non-obstructive path. You will see others for the Christ in them, which is the same as in you, and your relationships will start sharing this common ground.

Chapter 35

He Will Wait Till You're Ready

Letting go of the ego is easy. But it's not as simple as removing the tarp off the mint condition '57 Chevy sitting in the spare garage. Rather, it's more like peeling an onion back.

Since the separation and all ego-based fragmenting have compounded continually, the ego-based mind has layered itself tightly around the core of your true being. Why do we keep adding layers?

So-called Freudian theory dictates that our past is the seed that sprouts the present. Also, we've been taught that to heal the wounds of the past we must first go back to visit those old traumas. The therapy seems to be that we should remember them or even relive them so we may understand how our adult behavior has been caused by them.

Unfortunately, with this insight—or we can say "hindsight" into our past—is a tendency to assign blame. How often have we heard this or a similar song? "My mother was never around for me. She was always too busy and couldn't be bothered. Now I'm always striving for attention." Or, we may have heard this similar accusation: "My father was physically and emotionally abusive, so now I can't trust any man in an intimate relationship."

Supposedly this type of therapy that wants us to trace our disturbing history is said to free us, and brings us to being independent, self-actualized individuals, able to exist happily, completely on our own, loving ourselves and healing our "inner past." Having finally achieved this, we find that love follows, or at least that's what the ego tries to promise us.

However, your true *Self* doesn't need any final achievements, nor does it need to feel "actualized" in order to be happy. The Christ in you is only of joy and doesn't need "improvements" in order to know the happiness that exists within love and doesn't need to be "found" as if it were hiding behind something. There are no gaps in the Oneness of Love that could make room for a hiding place.

What you must do is *let go* of the illusion that is so tightly layered around you, that covers or obscures your vision. To try and penetrate this cover is an effort, a *cause* you wish to make. But *letting go* of it is an effect given to you by the true *cause* of love. It's the love for your innermost *Self.*

* * *

Many who have followed the therapeutic lessons or formulas of past soul searching wonder why they can't see beyond the body, to the beauty in those they try to forgive which helps the joy in relationships.

My own experience on the receiving end of an abusive relationship leading to a marriage I thought would be a "cure all," taught me that assigning blame does not bring healing, and the more I searched for my past, the more blaming I'd consume with myself. Forgiveness will show us how the pieces of the puzzle fit together, where blame merely only makes the glue that keeps the pieces stuck together in their old pattern. In this forgiveness—that overlooking by looking beyond ego-based thought—is loving and heals our interdependent connections with others in the present.

A good example in this is in a friend of mine who was contemplating a divorce with his wife, which he knew would be an ugly drawn-out drama mostly over money. He told me he had reached a point in his marriage with tremendous frustration, that he'd never be able to change his wife's manipulative pattern. This is when he jokingly commented that it was going to be "cheaper to keep her." He said he'd heard that line on a country song. Certain characteristics that annoyed him or enraged him or even at times what would hurt him would not cease. His illusion that changing her was possible lost the game. He truthfully asked himself: "How can I, or is it possible I can, love this woman beyond these flaws I've been seeing?"

Once he crossed that bridge between the fantasy of making change in her, to the reality of knowing it's not necessary because we all have our flaws, then my friend was able to see things starting to get interesting with a new ongoing excitement. Her manipulative behavior began no longer seeming to be manipulation, after all. He said to me, "That's when things finally became real, and when we both were able to love the realness and wholeheartedness in each other, then we were always laughing and having more fun than ever before."

People everywhere in their relationships, especially between men and women, have traveled different paths toward adulthood. Both sexes have ended up feeling wounded, cheated, and increasingly isolated. We cannot rewrite our developmental history by merely loving ourselves alone toward healing. Certain relationships bring about wounds, and their healing also requires other kinds of relationships. These can be heterosexual, homosexual, or nonsexual, but still love relationships in the act of kindness, mentoring, teaching, spiritual leadership, and a host of others that are necessary in close personal bonding.

* * *

It's no fantasy when you can imagine how beautiful those who you forgive will look, including yourself. Especially yourself. Nothing can ever be so lovely. In this you will witness the Holy Spirit busy at His task. This is why He was given to each of us in all walks of life, and all of His Teaching leads to seeing it.

This great feeling and loveliness that I experienced while writing this book was not a fantasy, even while mostly written from behind bars in prison. It is the real world where illusion is not sought after or made up. Nothing is needed to hide the truth, there is no reason to. The bridge between the world of illusion and the real world is so little and so easy to cross over because the truth in you is that easy to accept. Trying to hide it is what makes difficulty, along with anxiety and stress, which only add to any hardship.

Your acceptance of the absolute truth in all that you encounter in this world, including with yourself, is this strong little bridge. But you've been afraid of it. Take the step. It's the smallest you'll ever take that results in such a great accomplishment toward your participation in the Atonement, just as my friend Ed, who is doing a life sentence in prison is able to realize, and he has plenty of room for fun-loving joking around.

The real world is attained simply by complete forgiveness of the old world that you must *let go of.* It no longer exists in your mind, because it never did. This is why you must overlook it by looking beyond it, and only then will you have understood the real meaning of forgiveness. Talk is cheap, but looking beyond the ego in you and in others requires no such talk. Think about it.

How much do you really want salvation, which is your true free will? Only here can you live a life you truly desire and *want*, rather than *wishing* or what others wish for you. The Holy Spirit, who is a part of you in wholeness, is eager to give this to you. He does not want to wait, but He will wait in patience for you to be ready.

All you need to do is truthfully let Him know when you are ready.

Part IV

Holiness, the Real Goal in Your Relationships

Chapter 36

Seeing the Ego as the Culprit

What is the difference in meaning between your *brother/sister* and the *Christ* within?

Brotherhood shares the vision behind or beyond that tiny segment of separated mind that continues to dream of time, space, and form.

Christ is the real and whole unseparated *you* waiting for the dreamer to awaken and realize wholeness. Sounds pretty much the same as brotherhood, doesn't it? That's because you are one, with me, and united in wholeness.

It is your resurrection, and of your brother/sister, that Christ awaits with open arms, where all yearning for a split-mind has faded away, ceasing to exist. The Holy Spirit also of this *sameness of mind* gives reality to the process, just as He did with our elder brother, Jesus.

When I first introduced my ideas and my interpretations of the many principles of *A Course in Miracles*, I was met with enormous resistance. Many individuals, including some close to me, were not ready to accept these ideas. Some people thought that when I was throwing out the idea of the body as being real, that I was also throwing out the Bible. This is certainly not the case.

Once the "thinkers" of the group I'm talking about settled down and allowed themselves to look more closely and deeper into themselves, they had no choice but to accept the glimpses they'd always been getting of One-mindedness. They were seeing beyond the body all right, but were afraid to trust what was really there. They could see that God and Christ as one—not two—is all there is and is the only existence that is real. Anything else we think we see is either a projected image of separated thought or it is a reflection of our reality—Christ as within and one with God. This is the whole and complete real universe. Our age-old ideas and views about Divinity have left a question mark in all of us, and our thinking has changed radically, too.

That which has allowed individuals to accept in a nonthreatening way the simple message from my first book, *The Master of Everything*, was the manner in which it was presented. Every part was based on common and some uncommon experiences that had a uniting value. Those individuals who shared these types of experiences could immediately grasp these ideas. Even the uncommon, more unheard-of experiences, raised an honest eyebrow.

* * *

Often we're too dependent on others and their opinions. When we can experience the truth within ourselves, we're not so dependent on others to guide or teach us. With access to the truth within, we can release the need to rely on what others dictate to be the best way, and we can easily shift into what feels real for ourselves. You don't have to be threatened by differences, but rather welcome them and try to appreciate them. What appreciates, raises value?

When some so-called intellectuals attempted to debate me, I declined because I saw it was a waste of my time, plus I had no reason to prove my stance. I did, however, simply point out that my message is not for everyone. But in my own experience I suggested only what may be helpful to many individuals in all walks of life, regardless of formal education or chosen belief system.

When they demanded proof, as everyone would, I simply said my ideas were based on plain old truth which was common sense. These doubters were so used to the old way of depending on the approval of academic or church doctrine, that they couldn't conceive of something new, which was really not new at all coming from common sense. My ideas and findings were criticized for not being the result of an extensive study, with references or proven source material from multiple other claimed experts, who based their proof of their own studies and those of years and years gone by.

Believing only in theory that has been passed on down by generations is like waiting for a religious leader to say it's okay to use the Internet. Regardless of what we learn from the past, we must always put it to the test of our own real thoughts. This is where our real vision comes from. This is the new awakened awareness becoming of many other individuals today, who say they're not missing out on what feels real.

We're all open to different messages, but we seem to go with what is true for ourselves. We must look beyond by overlooking, first, well-meaning but misinformed family, friends, professionals, and others who are not absolutely sold for themselves about true reality, let alone how their own egos have dominated even the way they have learned to forgive. Or, we could say how they've not allowed their real inner guidance to show them what forgiveness truly is.

* * *

What if you begin overlooking your doubts by looking beyond them? If forgiveness is to overlook the actions of the ego by looking beyond it, couldn't we say that remembering only the loving thoughts we once gave and received is to forgive?

We can also realize this is an undoing from our memory of all other wrong-minded thoughts. The ego will call this denial. To *atone* is to undo where the only thing denied is the unreal. Forgiveness by looking beyond ego activity is the only way to undo the errors of obstruction, in order to reach Atonement. We can say that forgiveness is a selective remembering, but one not based on your selection alone.

However, we do see shadows of reality and then we project

images as being our enemy. The shadow takes on a figure of what we're really not, and then we think we forgive it. While ego-based thought makes grievances out of nothing, we seem to look at the real self within as needing our forgiveness.

Let me explain:

If you feel that I have wronged you, keep in mind it is my own ego and its behavior which is the culprit. But instead, you will seek to forgive my realness which is forever innocent. From behind the dream, I cannot be wrong-minded. The Christ in me has nothing to do with any such ego actions that you may see being carried out.

Therefore, try to see that your offering someone forgiveness is an offering you give to yourself, by looking beyond one's ego to the Christ within that you both share as one. It is important that you understand this totally before you continue in this book. But be sure to understand this in a way that is right for you. The truth in you is what is right for you. You'll know when you've seen the light.

Now you should know what is really meant when you say to someone you are close to, "I can't believe you could have acted this way, when surely I see you're a good person deep down."

By offering forgiveness from ego to ego all we make is a shadow figure of our real Self. That shadow becomes a projected image of what we think is our guilt. This is where illusion lives, in the shadow that you've made seem to be real. These shadows represent the wrong doings to you and you see them as real, but they are only as real as the dream. By keeping them hanging around in your sight, true forgiveness is never realized. It's not realized because you were not willing to "overlook by looking beyond the ego."

We seem to wish to carry these shadows at our sides so "just paybacks" may prevail, hoping the shadow has a witness to prove guilt of another without harming ourselves. The thinking seems to be "sooner or later he will get what he deserves," or, "one day she'll realize what goes around comes around."

These shadow appearances speak clearly for the separation. Only a separated thought system can hear or see them. They give us the *reasons* why we should enter into *unholy* relationships and call them "special" only to support the ego's goals and make relationships hail to its power which promises fantasy and is nothing.

Chapter 37

The Unholy Relationship Fades as It Is Questioned

The shadow figures have lived in our wrong-mindedness and have been fragmenting more and more thought for generation upon generation, and this is due to the lessons that try to prove the ego-based mind's interpretations as being holy.

This is so only in a way that the ego understands holiness. "Holier than Thou" has its own separate thought system that structures its beliefs. What we do to protect it we call love. Think of the things we do in the name of love. A parent prepares to strike his child and says, "This will hurt me more than it hurts you." But if you think about this, does the parent really believe this without guilt?

We project an image with a thought that shadows it speaking for vengeance, and every relationship the shadows enter only widens the illusion. These relationships take no exceptions in making their purpose anything but the truth about the other for your purpose.

This leaves you seeking an illusory purpose of fantasy. This is why it's so easy, then, to see in each other what is really not there, which ultimately you seek and justify revenge as rightfully due. This is where my friend could foresee an ugly divorce setting on the horizon if he didn't find another way of looking at the entire picture. After true contemplation he decided he really was not seeing a manipulative demeanor in his wife. Rather, it was he who was accepting the image he projected of her based on his desire to judge her.

How often have we heard of, witnessed, or been a victim of spousal abuse? Whether it is the victim or the spouse doing the abusing, quite often that same type of abuse, whether received or given, occurred in their childhood by a parent.

It seems whatever reminds us of past wrongdoings continues to attract us, but only seem to be of love and with the thinking: "This time it will be different."

It's the shadow, not reality that attracts us. Why? Because illusion is where the guilt is. Then the relationship becomes united through the body. I'm sure you're nodding your head in agreement if you're with me here, and seeing this in some of your own past relationships.

However, what you may not realize is the means that go into making the relationship unholy. One thing for certain is unholiness reinforces itself just as holiness does, and it does so by gathering to itself what it perceives to be like itself. Have you heard the saying; "Who's calling the kettle black?"

* * *

In the unholy relationship it's not so much the attraction you have of the body of who you attempt union, but it's more so for the bodies of those who are not there or not involved at all, yet. It's for the attraction you think you need of others, so that others might be attracted to you and your ability to make such an accomplishment in your new relationship.

This makes you known by others as you wish them to, so that you may hide even deeper your fears of rejection. Thereby, you continue with unlikely types of relationships while repeating the same process. Why? Because we're so desperate to seek the world's approval on just about everything we pursue in life, especially relationships.

Even the body of the other, which is already a severely limited perception made by a limited projection, is not the central focus. The focus is on what can be used of the relationship for your own fantasies, or for furthering more unreal projections that you wish to think are real and offer you a false sense of security. But with this tactic by the ego, more guilt is added to the pile. For some reason, we place value here.

What really is the unholy relationship? Basically at its foundation is ego trying to unite with ego. Every step we take in making and maintaining and even breaking off the unholy relationship is a move toward further fragmentation of ego-based thoughts with unholy motives. But unholy is *not* something like "skipping church services" this Sunday, but unholy is pretending to honor your Divinity. More and more shadow figures enter, and the Self you intend them to be in reality decreases in importance. You then will sense unnaturalness which you have allowed, and this piles on more guilt.

Time is cruel to the unholy relationship. The attraction of this relationship begins to fade as it is questioned. Being that you had some questionable doubts since it began, it had been fading all along.

Remember, we said much earlier that what is unreal never lasts. Same as the body. When the unreal is formed, doubt has its reasons for entering because its purpose is impossible. Well, at least it seems to be, or as the story goes since time began.

From here is where the Holy Spirit brings into play His interpretation of the body being used as a means of communication into relationships, where your ego's only purpose is fantasy with continued separation from true reality. He will look beyond separated thought. The Holy Spirit's only desire with separated thought or wrong-mindedness is to undo it.

If He can help you to let go of all but the loving thoughts, then what remains is the eternal. The past fades away and is transformed into the present, which cannot possibly conflict. Why? Because all that remains is only of the *now.* Nothing else.

* * *

Remember, reflection of your true reality doesn't come from darkness, but projection does. Reflection needs and has a Source, which is light. This is why we're able to continue in the present by increasing our awareness of it as always being *now*.

A value comes into play of our present moments. We learn to treasure them more. These become loving thoughts that spark a beauty that once would have been hidden away in what you would have seen as the ugliness of an unholy relationship. Yet, these present "now" moments turned loving thoughts, soon come to life as the relationship is given to the Holy Spirit, who shines light to beautify it.

This could entail simple greetings, like the person in a grocery store who asks you for directions in finding a particular food item. It doesn't necessarily mean the relationship of that moment or two need be developed further beyond that point. But it could. The point is that every meeting has something to give and receive, and is why it is a relationship on some level and is not meant to be unholy. They only become unholy because we make them a part of our separated thoughts that quickly become of the past, which is unreal. That is what the Atonement centers on, the undoing of the past where projections no longer exist and reflection takes over, allowing us to let go of separated thought.

But the ego-mind can seem to make letting go difficult because it seeks to resolve its problems by reliving them, then tries to convince you there can be no solution without some form of compromise. "Give and take," so to speak, is a sacrifice the ego will lure you into living by.

On the other side of things, the Holy Spirit wants only to make His resolutions complete and perfect without sacrifice of any kind, unless you call *letting go* of your ego-based thoughts a sacrifice. This is why your Teacher seeks and does indeed find the source of the problem, and in His undoing process will this separation of thought more and more become corrected by reversing it and true union of mind will be brought closer. Only then can your body experience true joy.

But keep in mind the Holy Spirit is not at all concerned by any reasons you may have for separated thought that only seem to exist. All He knows about separation is that it is unreal and must be undone, a reversal of your thought process. He will help you to begin reflecting your true thoughts instead of projecting thoughts you made up.

So when you allow the Holy Spirit to have complete control and uncover that hidden spark of beauty in any relationship, and open up your vision as He shows it to you, its loveliness will attract you. You will be unwilling to ever lose the sight of it again, and will be open for it in all others you encounter. By leaving yourself open, this spark will transform the relationship where more and more of it will come your way. It won't hide itself any longer.

By keeping yourself open to witness this spark of holiness in new and existing relationships, you are *not* in any fashion leaving yourself open to abuse, but the ego would like you to think so. This spark of holiness is safe and protected by the Oneness that you are with the holiness of creation itself, however hidden it might seem to be in your current relationships. This of course does not mean you shouldn't walk away from threatening-type behavior or call for help.

You must begin allowing yourself to notice the *reflective* light of Christ within them, their real *Self*, regardless of any brave ego-based front. This doesn't mean, either, that you must "bring home to mom" everyone you meet. It simply allows yourself to accept God in everyone, and the Holy Spirit brings them to you and you to them, because He knows of its reality and the purpose it is intended to serve, in order that you may live your true free will.

Simply give the past to Him and change your mind about it for yourself. But first try to realize how you arrived from the past to where you are now, and why.

Chapter 38

The Holy Relationship Is Real, Natural

When we meet someone for the first time, or run into an old acquaintance we haven't seen in a while, we choose to acknowledge them with a common greeting. "Hello, so nice to meet you." Even our everyday greetings to those we run into are usually only a few short words whether we're sincere or not, such as "Hey, what's up," or "Hope you have a fine day."

Usually these types of greetings acknowledge that there is a body or a personality we either do or don't get along well with, or who we're afraid of or shy to, or feel superior to. Often it's unreal.

In South African culture when people greet someone they can often be heard using the word "Sawabona." This word translates into, *I see "You,"* and not just I see your body. But it is, *I see "You"* with a capital "Y." in other words, "I see your true *Self*," or your true essence, or, the Christ in you.

Imagine what your life might be like if every time someone greeted you, and you greeted them in return, that it was always mutually a concern and a pleasure in seeing "You." The *Self* behind the dream of separation is Christ reflecting reality while you dream of bodily form.

If you don't know who others are, then you don't know who "You" really are either. If you're constantly judging others, you are lost in your own small, dreaming, judging self. When you see others as being small, you remain small. Your ego-based mind continues trying to hook itself deeper into the ego of others at the same time their ego tries to hook you.

* * *

We can say the ego is like a couch potato. It's used to lying around with the remote control, channel checking those same old reruns, which is its projection of life. More of the same is all you'll find on those familiar channels. In Mayberry, Andy is still the sheriff, with Barney as his devoted deputy and still up to his frivolous worrisome way. Just like on another channel, Archie Bunker is still screaming at the Meathead, and ordering Edith to "stifle." What can the other channels show us?

You must be willing to tune into a new live channel with clear reception that you probably have not known existed. Your ego-based mind will most always resist this. The ego's nature is its treasuring the familiar and the same old judgments handed down from a generation before. It thrives on conflict. It will draw you into it every chance it gets. The *Self*, however—your reality—is yearning for change. It wants happiness by tasting freedom. It knows that pure joy and freedom are its nature.

With your willingness to truly *see* other individuals as who they are from behind separation—beyond unreality and on a regular basis—you will soon begin to tune into channels of extending happiness, with secure and unfearful feelings that will not try to shut you off. You will leave behind the projections of reruns that never change. By tapping into the only real thought system that exists, the thoughts of your real *Self* will come forward, and others will see this about you.

Think about it. When we are truly happy, where does this elation emanate from? We will usually answer this by saying, "God gives us this elation," and this is correct. But let's look at this closer.

A Course in Miracles helps us here when it states, "God established His relationship with you to make you happy, and nothing you do that does not share His Purpose can be real."

Everything God created is a form of happiness, and all that is happy has the ability to extend further happiness. So if we take this a bit deeper, we can add that whatever does not create happiness cannot be real.

It's possible for us to be illusively happy, and in fact we're so good at this act we practice it all the time. The Holy Spirit doesn't see a task for depriving us of our special relationships, but He does assume the task of transforming them.

To transform is to have a change in nature or in your function from unreal to real. Learning comes from transformations. The Holy Spirit will restore to your special relationships the function which was given them by God. The function we've given them or made them out to be is clearly to make fantasy, and real happiness does not join there.

However, there is the *holy relationship* which is in line with God's Purpose, rather than, trying to force a substitute for it.

* * *

Anything that is holy has a function with wholeness as its foundation. Every special relationship you've ever made has been a substitute for what you truly want. You've placed your true free will on the back burner, so to speak, and have placed ego needs upfront.

Your true free will is certainly holy, because it's real. It is a free will that defines you truly and your definition is necessary to complete the whole Sonship, which is at full Atonement. This is what gives you real happiness. The illusive happiness you've been using to hide your guilt works only as an enhancement for this substitute which leads to ultimate turmoil.

Although we've been dreaming of separation, we've also made very real relationships. We often don't recognize them. Their substitutes sit on a pedestal and are valued so strongly that when truth calls to us as it does constantly, we answer with another substitute. Every special relationship we make has its basic purpose, which is to occupy our minds with fantasy so complete that we think it will protect us from the truth. We hide our fears of reality here. But what we don't realize is that we truly have nothing to fear.

Try to understand the special relationship as the ego's answer to the creation of the Holy Spirit, who is God's answer to the separation. At the beginning of time when we chose the dream of separation as being an identity separate from God, He wanted us to have His Spirit as our Guide all the way through the dream until its completion, as well as help us in a natural but certain awakening.

Although, aware of threat, the ego didn't understand what had been created. The ego frantically evolved with generation upon generation building a defense system to protect its separate identity, and became leery of voices in our hearts, or, the Holy Spirit. This is the ego-based mind's response to the gift given us to heal.

* * *

Consider when we heal, in whatever form that might be, the blessing of our own healing holds within it the truth about everything.

In reality, the truth is that the Holy Spirit is in close relationship with you, because in Him is your relationship with God—which never left you. The relationship you have with Him can never be broken, because the Holy Spirit who is a part of all of us cannot be separate. Therefore, through Him is where all your true relationships are preserved, and this is the part of you with me, and me with you, and that union is the *holy relationship*.

This *holy relationship* is where God's Purpose is preserved in each one of us, which can only be your true free will as well as mine.

Being threatened is what keeps the ego-mind on alert, and because a part of our mind has accepted the separation, or ego, this part of us is anxious to preserve its reason in the way it sees it. It cannot understand its own insanity, but is what you must realize in what it means to have you restored to sanity. Insanity protects its thought system, and its defenses are as insane as what it believes it needs to protect. The special relationship is the ego-based mind's most lucrative defense structure, thereby moving its insanity.

By now you should be realizing that the thought system the special relationship protects is merely a system of delusions. You are recognizing, at least in general terms, that the ego is insane. Yet, you still somehow seem to see the special relationship to be different. We have looked at it quite closer than we have about other aspects of the ego's thought system, which you are more willing to let go of. But this remains no different than the others, and as long as you hang on to the special relationship, you are accepting the ego as a separate whole.

Separation indicates something other than total Oneness of mind and can never truly become whole. Partial dedication to Truth is impossible. Think about it. What kind of relationships do you maintain?

Chapter 39

A Relationship with a Degenerate

In the *holy relationship*, you are constantly reminded of the experiences leading to the relationship becoming and evolving into what it is now. When you become aware of the *holy relationship* you will have taken a major step toward perceiving the real world. This can be a phenomenal lesson by the Holy Spirit. I'd like to share a lesson brought forward in me.

Here's a story about my longtime friend, Coleen, who I coincidently ran into after a lapse in time of about ten years. This was a period in my life when all hell was flaming and burning up all round me. This is when I'd been recently indicted by a grand jury and facing a prison sentence, but was not yet brought in by the authorities for the financial mess that would be a long drawn-out court fiasco, and prison ahead of me.

Coleen showed up surprisingly at a coffee shop one morning, much like a Star Bucks. I was contemplating my situation and debating my decisions as I stirred the clouds in my coffee, which were similar to the clouds in my mind. The surprise meeting was mutual as I first noticed her blonde hair tied up underneath a pink ball cap with her ponytail hanging out the back. Both of us smiled at each other with a surprised look, and as if we were mind reading each other, she walked over to my table and took a seat. We were both taken back.

Coleen grabbed my hand from across the table as she asked me so sweetly how I'd been doing. Neither of us was in a rush to get somewhere, so we both decided to do a bit of catching up, but only after she'd whispered to me about how often she thought of me. The coffee shop was fairly new and she thought she'd give it a first try. At one time the two of us were a strong item.

Coleen had just finished a book-signing tour around the region. I was surprised to find her an author. I'd always known of her as an art teacher. She and another schoolteacher coauthored the book with a topic on helping parents with troubled kids and their behavioral problems, the ones who carry their attitudes into the classroom.

The book uses art to help the kids who have no desire to learn. The book was rapidly becoming a success and she had much she wanted to tell me. Coleen and I, as described in an earlier chapter in this book, were close before, and how it was that we separated was just one of those things in a conflicting world. So I was extremely interested in her story, and also excited to be sitting across the table from her, especially at this point in my troubles, that she had not a clue about.

* * *

After about a full hour which only seemed like an instant, Coleen, of course, was devastated to hear about the business errors that most likely were sending me to prison. She gave me some kind words of encouragement that I still treasure today, and which I have incorporated into my mindset when I sit down to write. In fact, her generosity found its way inside the prison walls with her written letters of continued support. Coleen always closed a letter informing me of her will to help me wherever she could.

Back at the coffee shop during that delightful meeting, I had asked Coleen to expand on what prompted her to write the book. I also indicated my own desire to one day write, and this is something neither of us had known of each other when we were a "hot item."

She went on to tell me about her very first day of teaching high school many years ago, when she was fresh out of college with a brand-new teaching degree.

Her classes that day were going well, and she felt being a teacher was a dream come true. That was until the last period of that first day as a teacher of the sophomore class. Coleen said this is when she felt tested.

While she took a sip from her coffee, I could see she still had an excitement in her eyes about our chance meeting that morning. As she placed her cup down with her red lipstick marked on the rim of the cup, she began telling me about walking toward the classroom. She heard loud commotion that sounded like furniture crashing. As she opened the door to her classroom, she saw one boy on the floor on top of another boy, punching him. It was a school day fight for sure. "Listen to me, you degenerate," yelled the boy doing the punching. "Keep your hands off my sister! Do you hear me? The next time I see you near her, I'll put you in the hospital!"

Coleen described to me how she interjected with her tiny frame and sheepishly asked them to quit. Suddenly twenty-two pair of eyes were glaring on her. She knew she didn't sound convincing. Glaring at each other, and at her, the two boys slowly took their seats. Neither boy was hurt.

At that moment the teacher from across the hall, who was older and been teaching for many years, stuck his head in to make sure everything was under control. He shouted at the students to settle down and to respect and listen to their new teacher.

Coleen laughingly explained to me how powerless she felt. I shared in her laughs and we both looked at each other in awe, still how we hooked up that day "accidentally," when she corrected me to say it was coincidentally. Where did the time go and how long it had been since I'd last seen her, were my thoughts. It felt nice to be with her that morning. The feeling was certainly mutual.

* * *

Before Coleen continued to tell me more about her teaching debut, she excused herself and got up to use the restroom, but first she bent over and as she leaned next to me she slid her ball cap sideways so it wouldn't interfere with the small kiss on my forehead. I quickly thought, "Just like the Coleen of before."

I noticed she stopped by the waitress counter to mention a few words. The waitress smiled, went behind the counter to prepare a plate. While Coleen was still in the restroom the waitress delivered to our table a blueberry whole grain muffin, one for each of us. My favorite, Coleen remembered after all the years.

Upon returning to the table we both chuckled about the blueberry muffin and then she continued to tell me about how she tried to urge calmness into herself, but the anxiety in the classroom continued. The rest of that first day she was frightened of being a flop, but as the class was leaving for the day, she did make an authoritative move.

Coleen told me she detained the one boy causing the trouble whose name was Jeff. She warned Jeff that punching another student was uncalled for in her classroom. "Lady, don't waste your time," Jeff blurted bitterly. "We're the degenerates of this school and we do what we wish." The teenage boy turned his back and stomped out of the classroom in disrespect. Jeff was the gang leader type who the others followed.

She described how she slumped down in her chair and began wondering if being a teacher was really meant to be. She began talking to herself about leaving teaching all together. She started thinking that she'd give it till the end of the school year and suffer it out to take the summer break where she'd have time to find something more rewarding rather than conflicting.

"They got to you, didn't they?" these were the kind words of the older teacher from across the hall that popped his head in earlier, and now hoping to lend an ear. Coleen, of course, nodded with agreement. "Don't worry," he said. "I taught many of them in summer school. There are only twenty-two of them and most will never graduate anyway. Don't exert too much energy with the bad ones. Just focus on the good ones with potential who you can help."

I couldn't keep my mind off how Coleen seemed not to of aged at all since I'd last laid eyes on her, which was some ten years ago when we went to a Billy Joel concert at the old Richfield Coliseum. This and more reminiscing thoughts were twirling in my memory as I thought of the song "She's Got a Way about Her."

As Coleen stirred some sugar-free sweetener in her coffee, she added that for several weeks ahead she would continue having problems in that class, especially with Jeff. She said she'd never forget the look on his face as he said with a proud disgust that "we're the degenerates." That bounced around in Coleen's mind about how those kids were looking at themselves.

* * *

Coleen told me of an idea that dawned on her with how to handle the situation with the so-called Degenerates, which really caught my attention as being brilliant. One day in class she made intentional eye contact with each student, the good ones as well as the bad ones. Then she went to the chalkboard and wrote "neeloc."

"This is my name," she said. "Can anyone tell me what it says?" they laughed and went on to tell her the name was "weird," and that they'd never seen such a word before. She went back to the board again to this time write "Coleen." Several of them anxiously answered out the word and gave her a funny look.

"You are correct," she said, "My name is Coleen." She grabbed their attention with a little story about herself. "I was a learning-impaired child for most of my school years. It's called 'Dyslexia.' When I began school, I couldn't write my own name. It was extremely difficult for me to learn how to spell, and numbers seemed to swim in my head. I guess you could call me a 'Degenerate,' too, right?" Coleen told me how she can still see the sense of shame in their faces, and Jeff hanging his head the lowest as though he was hiding.

A few of the kids went on to ask her how and why she became a teacher, with having had her own learning problems. Her response was how she hates to see people being labeled, and she knew she wasn't stupid and had a desire to learn. She continued to convince these young teenagers that her class was going to be a way of helping them to learn, and to let go of their own label on themselves as being *degenerate*. She told them she would not allow any degencrates to be involved with her classes.

Coleen looked across the table at me smiling as she said how the months flew by, and the improvement with her students as a whole was wonderful. It seemed some of them would help the others who were having a problem in particular areas. Her elation, even of something from the past, was enough to lift my spirits about what I was facing.

She said she caught glimpses of Jeff's improvements when he boasted about his interest in the novel, *To Kill a Mockingbird*, and the excitement he showed for his own accomplishment of reading such a book in its entirety. Suddenly Coleen realized she had the whole class doing well, and with interest, awe, and enthusiasm to want more. She was sorry to see that school year come to an end. She was thrilled that these futurc adults had taken a liking to their art and English teacher.

These students were so fond of her, Jeff headed up a few of the other boys to help him with a task. The boys convinced a local funeral home to donate several flower arrangements left over from a funeral, that otherwise would be thrown to trash. The boys with Jeff leading the way walked into the classroom on the final day of school and presented Coleen with beautiful flowers. As she told me about this occasion I could see her eyes tear filled. I reached over the table and placed my hand on hers. We both looked at cach other and simply laughed about how, after all this year, here we were, in a way still together.

* * *

After telling me that her Siamese cat that she named *Laz*, a kitten when I'd last seen Coleen, was still alive, doing well, but a bit slow, we continued to enjoy our time together as we sipped on our coffee.

She continued telling me more about the students, and that when two more years had gone by, all twenty-two of the students graduated. In fact, six of them earned some form of college scholarships. Coleen had left the area to teach at a well-known art institute in New York for a few years, but now was back to stay. This is where she says she needs to be. Coleen was teaching for years, and for some reason never mentioned this story to me before, when we were involved. I guess there never was a good reason for her to bring it up.

However, after many years of teaching school, Coleen went back to that same high school which gave her that first teaching accomplishment. Only now there is a new building with increased attendance and state-of-the-art educational departments. "Nothing like when we went to school," she added.

The punch line here is incredible to her story. Jeff's son is in her sophomore English class, and, to boot, Jeff himself occupies a position in the school as *dean of boys*, which is close in line to the principal. Jeff holds a teaching degree and has earned his way up the ladder in the school system. She also told me Jeff has been the school's wrestling coach for seven years now, a position he will not give up, and the team has won several league championships.

I about dropped my coffee when Coleen told me this. She went on to add how she often laughs when she recalls the end of her first day as a teacher, a day she considered quitting for something more rewarding. "But wait," she said to me with her eyes peering into mine, "there's more," as her hand was squeezing mine from across the table. "You won't believe this," she said.

I sipped my coffee in anticipation and listened as she told me that Jeff is the coauthor of "their" book, targeted at parents with struggling teenagers. "What an inspiring story," I immediately whispered to her across the table with my head leaning forward and tears in my own eyes. Then she added, "I can't believe I never told you this before, I mean, the part about my rough start as a teacher."

The *chance* meeting that day with Coleen is still a fun memory, and the thought that I could have gone to a different coffee shop that day surely boggles my mind.

She has written to me on occasion while in prison and always closed with a few sentences that helped keep my enthusiasm alive about my own writing projects. Coleen is the only person I've known that not only includes a short "P.S." at the end of her letters, but also adds a brief "P.P.S.," and I've often borrowed this concept in my own letter writing.

I certainly hope this true story about my longtime friend and me clearly proves to you the "doings" and the "undoings" of the Holy Spirit through relationships. In all aspects of the *holy relationship*, as it begins, and into its developing stages, it is the reversal of the *special relationship* being a direct result of the Holy Spirit using it for His Purposes, by using time.

His goal replaces yours in the relationship. But keep in mind, His goal is always your true free will which develops into your purpose, displayed by your function in this world. We can say this is where your function is created whole, because it shares the function of the whole Sonship.

Chapter 40

The Goal Has Already Been Set

When many individuals think of spirituality, they will immediately think of their relationship to organized religion, such as the Catholic Church, the Protestant Church, Judaism, Islam, etc.

Although organized religion can nurture a deep and profound spiritual life, religion and spirituality are not necessarily the same. Sometimes they lead us to see the same things, but they are often very much different. We must recognize in ourselves if we are using religion, or is religion using us, to defend a separated thought system.

Dr. Naomi Rachel Remen suggested that "religion can be a dogma, a set of beliefs about the spiritual, and a set of practices which arise out of those beliefs."

We all know of the many religions in the world today, and they tend to be or think they are exclusive. But there truly is no religion that holds a special copyright on the spiritual, where its rules and laws of practicing faith try to convince us that "their way is the only way." Yet the spiritual is inclusive. It is the deepest sense of belonging, awareness, and participation. All of us participate in the spiritual at times, whether we realize it or not. Yes, even in a coffee shop where a "chance meeting" takes place.

There is no place we can go where we can be apart or separated from the spiritual, so perhaps one might say that the spiritual is that realm of human experience, which religion attempts to connect us through its dogma and practice. Sometimes it seems to be where the emphasis is on the body, rather than unity of mind. Religion is a bridge to the spiritual, but the spiritual lies beyond religion. Unfortunately, in seeking the spiritual we may become attached to the bridge, or ever chained to it, instead of crossing over it.

But I've discovered with myself that my own Catholic upbringing can now be experienced without the chains and in a new light. My connection to Catholicism now is more of a fellowship, and I can use my Catholic faith to deepen my spiritual oneness with an understanding of who and what I am.

Rather than feel governed or dictated by the Catholic religion I chose to remain involved with, it is "I" who decides where my spiritual life is leading me. For me, going to Catholic mass no longer is a defense or a commitment in proving my love for the Divine. In other words, I don't feel I have to prove to anyone about the reality of my faith. This is what frees me and allows me to openly discuss my faith, if I choose to do so. I know that I am of the Divine, and this knowledge is all I need, whether I go to mass and take the sacraments or not.

Your faith is a relationship, and just like all holy relationships it doesn't need to be defended. When we make a defense, it is essential that it do what it must in order to defend. This leads to a belief that is not wished for or wanted, but is more like a demand. We need to lighten up without defenses where our naturalness leads the way.

When unwishful changes enter into situations that are the grounds for relationships, this makes the relationships seem to be disturbed. But *what* you truly *want* can change this pattern and the disturbance fades away. What I mean, here, is, let's wake up to what we truly want and not what others prescribe. Your true *wanting* is where your faith lives while your real *Self* rises to your memory and joins the whole of creation. Your purpose then comes to the surface.

* * *

With defensiveness in any relationship, it will be out of line with its intended goal, and clearly not suited to the purpose that has been accepted for it. This is an unholy condition due to your own self-made goal being the only goal as you perceived it, in which it seemed to have meaning. Now you seem to see it making no sense.

Many relationships will break apart at this point, and the pursuit of the old goal is often reestablished in another relationship. But once you accept the goal of holiness, the unholy special relationship can never again be what it once was. You can't replace it. The role of truth will outperform the unreal or fantasy, and real joy is achieved. But the ego's anxiety is raised, becoming extremely intense with this shift in goals from fantasy to truth.

The ego becomes more frightened than its normally fearful state, and panic sets in. The relationship is changing, but not yet honestly enough to make its old goal completely unattracted to it. What will happen is its structure becomes threatened by the recognition of the urge for meeting a new purpose. The ego is uncomfortable and unaware of how to handle its thoughts.

Next, conflict will occur between the goal and the structure of the relationship, and it is so apparent that they cannot coexist. Yet the goal surely now will not be changed. Set solidly in unholy relationship, there is no course except to change the relationship to fit the goal.

*   *   *

Once a change is seen and accepted as being necessary as the only way out of this conflict, the relationship will continue to be severely strained.

The first thought might be to shift the goal more slowly, but this won't work because its contrast would be obscured. This would be giving the ego time to reinterpret each slow step according to its liking, making more fragmented thoughts. Only a radical shift in purpose could introduce a complete change of mind about what the whole relationship is intended to be for.

As this change develops and is finally accomplished, you will benefit increasingly with joy. But at the beginning the situation may be experienced as dangerously lacking substance.

A relationship between individuals for their unholy purposes suddenly will now have *holiness* as the goal. As the parties involved contemplate the relationship from the point of view of this new purpose, they nervously become appalled. Their perceptions of the relationship may even become quite disorganized. Yet the way in which it was previously organized no longer perceives serving a purpose they have agreed to meet.

This is where faith comes into play. You've allowed this goal to be set for you, and that alone was an act of faith. But don't abandon this faith because its rewards are being introduced. If you originally believed the Holy Spirit was there to accept the relationship, why wouldn't you still believe that He is there to purify what He has taken under His Guidance?

The goal has been eternally set. The situation has sanity as its purpose, but for now you're finding yourself in an insane relationship, which is being reorganized in order to arrive at the light of its goal.

Chapter 41

Don't Deny Yourself the Benefits

The previous chapter is intended to stir your thinking with a goal of bringing forward in your mind a sense of belonging, and not to throw you aloof.

Now you can realize that out of fear and for survival reasons, the ego will tempt you to substitute your turmoil, strained relationship, for another one in which you think the former goal can be achieved. You'll begin thinking that you can only escape from your distress by getting rid of the situation or a particular relationship with an individual. But you don't want to part ways entirely if you choose not to do so, that is, if you are willing to exclude major areas of fantasy from your involvement. For example, consider money:

The dream for more money seems to be a fantasy that one day may make your marriage complete. This couple seems to think if they only have *more* money, then they'd have the time they always wished to spend together. Please, help me out here, you've got other examples, I'm sure. Isn't it when they do get the time or the money, then it's something else lacking?

Do you see the fantasy that can be let go of in this picture? Letting go of it is what will save your sanity and provide for a lasting and loving relationship. It's not the money; it's the fantasy thoughts of the money that is the root to all evil.

Consider having faith in the Holy Spirit who led you to this relationship. He's not misguided you, as He understands what it is that you want. But you must give Him your faith a little longer, even in a confused and desperate state of mind. This will pass, and you will see the rewards of your faith emerge.

This is no different from Coleen's story about her teaching career. We saw her relationships along the way, and that she didn't abandon the Holy Spirit with a goal being left unmet. We were able to see what did result by Coleen with her faith, regardless of the rough start at teaching, in the lives of others and in their own successes that are ongoing today, let alone the lives they touch and so on.

Whatever it is you don't understand, gladly accept that you don't understand and let it be explained to you while you perceive His Purpose in the works of being holy. Remember, holiness is the *backbone* of your true free will. You will find many opportunities to blame someone or some situation for the failure of a relationship, because it will seem at times to have no purpose.

A sense of lacking direction may haunt you and remind you of all the ways you once searched for satisfaction and thought you found it. But don't forget, in *that* that itself is the misery you really found by trying to breathe life into your failing, so that you might make yourself into something you're not. By realizing this relationship has not been disrupted, it is saved.

* * *

Earlier we discussed that salvation means having the freedom to be who and what you truly are, and not what your failing and searching ego, or the world, tries to make out of you. You're waking up now to your own Divinity and you get some help from whichever bridge you choose to get you there. What you call this bridge is not important. But you are new at operating this way and may think you're lost. Your way might be lost, but don't consider it your loss. Too many ego-based variables placed you there.

It's extremely urgent that in your new way, now, you remember that you and the world have started over, but this time you're working together hand in hand at only the real. So don't be afraid to "take the bull by the horns," and walk the bull along your road that doesn't have the fears you once made for yourself by trying to achieve fantasy.

Your true free will is not fantasy. There is no such thing as a fantasy life. You must step toward the goal that has been set for you and remains unchanged. It's been waiting for you. The only way to arrive at the goal is to begin living it. By doing this you will have invited the Holy Spirit into the relationships that will get you closer to the goal. The groundwork is being laid. Otherwise, He would not have entered. Of course, you've made some mistakes, but you have also made enormous efforts to help Him at His Task, by your errors.

Try to understand that the Holy Spirit appreciates the growth in you for all that you've already done for Him. What He appreciates is value, and your mistakes are not seen as real to Him because they're overlooked. In other words, forgiven.

So now that you accept the fact that the Holy Spirit has forgiven you, this means you've also forgiven yourself. Ask yourself, have you been similarly grateful to others? Have you consistently appreciated your good efforts, and overlooked ego-based behavior? Or, are you blaming others and situations which will give you a lack of gratitude and make you unable to enter as well as appreciate a holy instant? You know, increase its value, yes? This expands your alertness of the eternal; otherwise, you lose sight of it all together.

The experience of the holy instant, however, is compelling but can be easily forgotten if you allow time to close over it. You must keep it in your awareness of time, but not concealed within it. The holy instant always remains. So where are you, now?

When you give true thanks to others you are appreciating a holy instant, because the results are being shared. To attack someone is not losing the instant, but it does make it powerless in its effects. Attack is not a true *cause.*

Just like my friend Coleen did, simply start recognizing the gifts you freely give the world and you'll be willing and able to accept the effects of the holy instant and use them to correct your errors while freeing yourself from their results. But certainly begin *seeing* yourself free, and do not deny yourself the benefits.

Chapter 42

Allowing Him to Relate through You

We've learned that each one of us is an integral aspect of the birthless, deathless, eternal, One-minded life of all that exists. As one, we are creation. But is this to say we share in each other's problems, struggles, pain, and turmoil that this world of form and separate identities has to offer us?

This world has often tried to impress on us that "It is better to empathize rather than to sympathize." But when we do empathize, are we not joining in their pain?

Nothing more than a bundle of thoughts that have separated or split away from that of the Oneness we share as our Source, the ego in its insanity, interprets empathy for its use in forming its own oneness, called the *special relationship*. Do we really wish to share in someone else's pain? Why do we think it's the thing to do? It's the ego in each of us that wishes we think this is what "glues" relationships together, and it does glue them but in no way creates them. The ego sees that sharing in another's suffering is a way to win over another's weakness, and then proceed building a relationship on *that*.

* * *

The ego-based mind wishes you to think the Holy Spirit's way is difficult because it's different. The Holy Spirit can use empathy to its maximum in His way if you'll allow Him to. His way certainly is much different from what the ego could ever dream up. Only the thoughts you have that are separate from God can experience the illusion of suffering.

Since the Holy Spirit is God, and is also you, He is the aspect of your mind that is never separate. This aspect in your mind does not recognize suffering. This is your wholeness—your real existence—and anything else is a self-made projection, an illusion that is part of time and space. But because of guilt the ego has us so overwhelmed with the body and bodily thoughts, that we often don't recognize true reality.

The Holy Spirit certainly is within you, but He is not dreaming along with you about your separated self. He does, however, constantly guard over your thoughts as you dream—and He guides you in a direction of thought that carefully awakens you, but only as He sees it fit for the benefit of the whole Sonship—which is you. In His Task, is the *cause* to the *effects* of the ego's gradual fading away?

As time ticks away and with the Holy Spirit's use of it, the ego-based mind fades in a sequential manner comparable to your awakening. Likewise, the more you awaken so does all of humankind open its eyes as a whole. In this awakened vision is where your holy relationships exist.

In this we can say the Holy Spirit doesn't join in your pain, but He understands that healing cannot be accomplished by gluing fragments together. This type of a "band-aid" state of mind, at best, may scar and still leave room for separateness. Why would the Holy Spirit want to share in this delusion? Since He is you, how can you expect a relationship to be true under this "glued-together" idea? But the Holy Spirit is involved in a continuous effort to heal your pain by bringing you into wholeness through your true free will, where pain is nonexistent. As the ego in you fades, wholeness is all that remains.

* * *

Empathy as the ego uses it is destructive by its deception, and the ego uses it only for particular types of problems with particular people. The ego will select these factors based on its ability to

216

prey on them with its goal of strengthening itself. When the ego identifies with what it thinks it can possibly understand, it tries to use the situation and increase itself by sharing the aspects that are like it. This is the ego's attempt to empathize so to weaken, and any attempt to do this is to attack.

This attempt has a goal of further fragmentation, and this splitting apart of mind and thought obscures the light of true reality. The real life is not seen. With this lack of vision, we don't understand what true empathy means. But we can be sure that if we calmly and quietly listen and allow the Holy Spirit to relate through us, we will automatically empathize with strength. We'll gain in strength but not in weakness. So how do you calmly listen? What's involved?

Consider again the story with my friend Coleen, the teacher. She was able to see that the students who called themselves "Degenerates" were stuck with an identification problem. She empathized by being willing and ready to see herself in them, due to her childhood learning disabilities, which she was able to overcome. Simply by Coleen sharing this with those particular students, she didn't share in their pain, but she did shine her light onto an idea for them to escape their own self-labeling, which was their pain.

We've learned that the wholeness of your true mind is infinite and eternal. The fragmenting mind will ultimately fade away, fragment by fragment until it experiences its end. You can look at this on a personal level with your own life and your life's situations and relationships, as well as seeing this on a larger scale with the entire world you project around you. It is the end of separation as well as the end of time.

One thought system is of projected images onto a screen you call your life. And with time the images gradually become blurred. The other thought system is real and its true thought that is continuously extending inward, where time and space and form have never truly existed.

Which thought system runs your relationships?

Chapter 43

Allowing Wholeness to Heal

You may say that the authentic, holy relationship sounds like something you want to have. So you ask me to give you a good example of what you can do to have these traits that attract this holiness. I'm going to help you find the answer.

A friend of mine told me of a contractor she'd recently met—a virtual stranger—who impressed her so much that she gave him a large remodeling job without even seeking competitive bids. He had a profound and attractive sureness. She later asked herself, what else was it that made her retain him? He seemed secure, focused, and without artifice. He cast off an *essence* which was clearly intelligence. That too made her think he was dependable. It was much more than his professionalism.

Some ancient texts suggest that the spiritually mature emit the light that's in them so that others may notice it. Abraham Maslow described self-actualizing adults as somehow "close to their own nature," childlike and transparent yet simultaneously stable, mature, and seemingly reliable. This fully functioning person is also at ease:

"What normally takes effort ... is done without any sense of striving, of working or laboring, but comes of itself." Maslow added, "One sees then the appearance of calm sureness and rightness, as if they knew exactly what they were doing, and were doing it wholeheartedly, without doubts, equivocations, hesitations, or partial withdrawal ... The greatest athletes, artists, creators, leaders, and executives exhibit this quality when they are functioning at their best."

I have often observed healthy and dynamic intensity in truly holy relationships. They're fully present. They listen and respect what's happening—with all their forces, their partner, their entire being. When problems arise, which they always will at times, they remain calm, they're relaxed, but as *A Course in Miracles* puts it, "… ready."

* * *

The miracle is simply the lifting away of the obscurity that prevents your true light from revealing the best each situation has to offer, and then moving forward. Creating miracles is an experience as you become more aware of the false projections made by the ego-based mind. Some people will struggle and place effort into having motivation and then wonder why some people are nasty to them, or that things never seem to work out for them. There are many reasons for this. Your failed past is not what governs your relationships with the outer world.

It could be people are mean to you, or the cards don't seem to fall your way, because you're not following your heart's desire. Your true free will is everything, and anything else the world will resist.

You may be swimming upstream with everything in your life, so of course life will be more difficult. It could also be you've been drawn to difficult and conflicting people in your life in order to teach you what it is you need to know, so you can let go of all this unnatural nonsense. You see, often when our hearts want to grow, we are attracted to situations that will challenge us and make us stronger and bring forward our inner desires. There are a variety of factors that determine our outer world and some obstacles which we have no control over.

Things which are real and things which are illusive have no connection to one another, other than how you wish to connect them. Illusive patterns always seem to try and connect to one another's likeness, but never form true wholeness.

Truth is always the unalterable one and same truth and doesn't require any such searching for unity. It is what it is. Truth and illusion each will unite with their own kind as a thought system, but they are totally separate and disconnected to each other. Illusion tries to attach itself but falls to the wayside. Illusion will, however, fade as it draws closer to the truth if you're willing to let it go. By perceiving there is a chance of the truth and illusion to coexist as true reality is your belief in separation, and it's why you need healing.

To understand healing and our personal life responsibility, it is important that we do not conclude that everything is a result of past conflict. It's time to update our thinking with open minds and open hearts that can consider many ideas and possibilities, and take action without fear, at once. It is important to recognize in this age that miracles are indeed real, and that belief which prevents you from feeling good about yourself is not a real belief.

True inspiration can only come from what is real. This is a time of needing great ego-based mind *house cleaning* for the entire world. It's up to you to initiate this new vision because it's conflicting wrong-minded ways are in your projected images. In fact, it's what makes these projections only seem to be real.

* * *

Even two thousand years ago Jesus taught that it was time to clean out the things that really do not serve us, and to create more room for the new ideas and beliefs that can serve a new potential.

As he traveled throughout the land, Jesus was increasingly troubled by signs that very few among his audience truly understood what was going on in their minds. This is why over and over again, through parables he was able to deliver his message in a way they could understand. But many of them still didn't understand, and throughout time much of his word became wrong-mindedly interpreted. Jesus called for nothing less than a drastic upheaval—or a revolution in human behavior—and he urged it right away in the present moment of spiritual crisis.

Here is how Jesus demanded individuals to open their minds: "You have heard it said an eye for an eye and a tooth for a tooth.

But I say to you, do not resist one who is evil. If anyone strikes you on the right check, turn to him the other also; and if one would use and take your coat, let him have your cloak as well; and if anyone forces you to go one mile, go with him two miles." Here Jesus is specifically referring to staying with another until he is able to witness illusion fade before the truth. With your presence he will see the Light. But, again, ego thoughts don't see it this way, and interprets only of the body and for the body.

Again and again Jesus encouraged faith beyond the body by overlooking it:

"Ask, and it will be given you; seek and you will find; knock, and it will be opened to you ... Look at the birds of the air, they neither sow nor reap nor gather into barns, and yet your Heavenly Father feeds them. Are you not of more value than they?" (In other words, have you considered your own true free will?)

And just a few more here, so the idea truly sinks in: "Why are you anxious about you, even Solomon in all his glory was not arrayed like one of these. But if God so clothes the grass of the field, which today is alive and tomorrow is thrown into the oven, will He not much more clothe you, O men of little faith? ... But seek first His kingdom [meaning your real *Self*] and His righteousness [the truth in you], and then all these things shall be yours as well."

By opening our minds to this you will come to know your true abundance. The body cannot be healed before the mind. When we understand and accept this we will be whole and the separated ego-based mind will have faded away.

*   *   *

If you catch yourself in the middle of an ego-based situation where you're realizing its building a *special relationship*, the best thing you can do is not try to hurt or heal it in your own way, because the ego will sneak in the back door on you. You don't want this to happen and you don't know how to accomplish healing on your own, or for that matter you don't truly know what it is. All any of us do know about empathy is what we've learned from the past, which really never existed.

The past is the projected image of what your ego thought it was. *Wholeness has no past* and that is why it heals. The fading of whatever is separated is healing. It's truly that simple. Therefore, there is nothing from your past you need to keep. To the ego-based mind, Jesus's messages and teachings we've just discussed were of many years ago, the past. But to your real *Self*, it occurred in this instant. How so? you surely ask. Does time truly exist in a dram, such as in all those years ago? Only if you're still dreaming will years seem like years.

The ego's thinking is to use empathy to make the real, and to keep it real. But you can simply step aside and let your fragmented thinking become absorbed like a sponge, *cleaned up by wholeness* where it will be healed for you.

The following is an excellent set of words for you to keep in mind, or they can be used as I do, for a prayer, whenever you might be tempted to judge any situation. For me, much like a good Catholic boy retains in his mind, the *Hail Mary*, I've also stored these words in my mind and bring them forward as I need them.

"I know I'm not alone, and do not want to intrude the past on my Guest, the Holy Spirit, Who shares my whole mind with me as One Mind. He is within me for my Purpose and I must not interfere."

The Holy Spirit knows how to deliver empathy on your behalf. He will place it in your heart. You will begin learning His interpretation of it if you will use your strength of truth, and not see the use of weakness. Simply accept His knowledge as your strength and be humble. You will know what to do.

Remember, the meaning of love is lost in any relationship that looks to weakness and hopes to find it there. The real power of love comes from the strength of your own knowledge about the truth in you. Only you would know of it. You can try all you wish but the stress and anxiety you will receive will prove you cannot fool yourself. Simply allow the truth to be as it already is within you, and don't try to force any magic on this. Don't let interpretations based on guilt and fear dictate your vision.

Jesus once said of a brother who asks even a foolish thing of you, to go ahead and do it. But He didn't mean to do a foolish thing that would hurt either of you. What hurts one, hurts the other. Foolish requests are foolish merely because they arise out of conflict. This is so because they also contain some element of thinking that we are *special*. But the Holy Spirit will recognize foolish needs as well as the real ones. He will teach you how to meet both without losing either or harming yourself.

On your own with ego-based thinking you'll try to do this in secrecy, and that is why you keep things separate and secret in your relationships. But this certainly is not Truth. No needs will be left unmet for very long if you leave them all to the Holy Spirit, Who wants to fulfill them.

He will not meet them secretly, because your needs are very necessary for the whole Sonship and not only for part of it. Thereby, try to see it in a way that makes perfect sense: The Holy Spirit wants what is best for each involved in your relationships, because He *is* each of you.

Afterword

When we try to understand miracles like those Jesus performed, the one's we've read about, we're met with an initial difficulty. The difficulty is in defining a miracle because we've never truly understood the real meaning of Christ.

What may be considered a miracle in one time period or in one society is commonplace in another. Even a hundred years ago people would have regarded as a miracle to be able to sit in a room and look into a glass-fronted frame and see plays being acted, actual theater, games being played, events from around the planet and beyond happening. Now, television is everywhere.

A Viking would have regarded an 80,000-ton steel ship speeding across the Atlantic Ocean as a miracle. A Roman charioteer would have regarded as a miracle an airplane, a jet, and the space shuttle. Hippocrates or Galen or any other ancient physician would have regarded modern anesthetics along with modern surgery like with the heart, lungs, and other organs, and transplants as a miracle. Julius Caesar or Hannibal, Napoleon or Wellington would have regarded as a miracle, even if it be a devilish one, the devastation of a nuclear bomb and other killing devices and methods.

However, within that same uninterrupted instant of the dream of separation where time only seems to be real, let's put this in another context. The conception of "the possible" does not stay steady. It varies from dreamer to dreamer and from age ancient to age new, both an unreality. For now, the dream advances. Are we ancient to those of five hundred, a thousand, or more years from today?

Let's not forget that while we reflect from reality the

separated mind will project its images, and every day we perform as a matter of course—based on love or fear—with no middle ground, which is of truthfulness or falsity, actions which previous generations would have regarded as fantastically impossible. We travel through the sky at 500 miles per hour and better, without thinking much about it. It's no longer the same *awe* it once was. We enter a hotel and are whisked up to the nineteenth floor and higher in an elevator. What would an elevator have meant to Sir Isaac Newton? We pick up a little instrument and carry on a conversation with someone thousands of miles away.

What would have been impossibility in one century is a routine action in the next. What would have been seen as a miracle in one age of history is a commonplace in another. Yet miracles are only needed while we dream of time. In eternity they do not exist.

In ancient times very few people had ever tasted fresh fish unless they lived fairly close to the sea. In many ancient ages it was considered as a luxurious delicacy. It was impossible to transport it any distance and keep it fresh in transit. But the dream continued.

To define a miracle as something which is impossible is a quite inadequate definition. Who is to define the possible in any way which is not relative to his own position in time and in progress? Remember, the holy instant remains infinitely wrapped around time.

If we are able to realize Christ as within the holy instant, and Jesus merely of time, then we can see the miracles of Jesus as the strength of Christ, but in time. We might see his miracles as the mental images projected of that time period and the spiritual climate in which they occurred. Since that is so, certain facts are based on interpretations that evolved from the New Testament, which must be taken into account.

The age had a completely different attitude toward the miraculous. Modern man is suspicious of anything he cannot explain, and he thinks that he knows so much about the universe and its working order that he will say roundly that miracles do not happen. The last thing man of today expects is a miracle.

On the other hand, the ancient world reveled in the miraculous. It looked for miracles; and the result was that apparently miraculous events occurred. To put this paradoxically, yet truly, the miraculous was a commonplace.

Can we say that your knowledge, now, and mine, that has come forward in our minds about the *holy relationship* is a miracle? Can we also say that real and holy relationships which you cherish, are seen in the holy instant, wrapped around time as miracles you created?

Yes, your holy relationships are the results of your miracles created by the Christ within—your true and real *Self*—and seeing time within the "instant" that is your existence. The goal from here until time's end is that this will be the commonplace. Once this happens, and it is everywhere, time will be no more, and the miracle no longer needed. Christ will rest as one just as He always has, because separation will have faded away—where we've healed and have totally awakened.

God Bless

Your brother in the holy instant

Jim Nussbaumer

References

Barclay, William. *The Mind of Jesus*. HarperCollins, 1960.

Casarjian, Robin. *Houses of Healing: A Prisoner's Guide to Inner Power and Freedom*. Lionheart Press, 2008.

Colson, Charles W., and Harold Fickett. *The Good Life*. Tyndale House Publishers, 2006.

Corneau, Guy. *Lessons in Love: The Transformation of Spirit through Intimacy*. Holt, 1999.

Covey, Stephen R. *The 7 Habits of Highly Effective People: Wisdom and Insights From*. Running Press, 1989.

Cranston, S. L., and Carey Williams. *Reincarnation: A New Horizon in Science, Religion, and Society*. Theosophical University Press, 1999.

Dimitrius, Jo-Ellan. *Reading People*. Ballantine Books, 1998.

Dreher, Diane. *The Tao of Inner Peace: A Guide to Inner and Outer Peace*. Harper Perennial, 1991.

Gray, John. *Practical Miracles for Mars and Venus*. HarperCollins, 2000.

Gunther, Max. *The Luck Factor*. Macmillan, 1977.

"John 4:16." *Bible*, New International Version ed.

Maslow, Abraham H. *Toward a Psychology of Being*. D. Van Nostrad Company, 1962.

"Matthew 7: 24–27." *Bible*, King James Version.

Pipher, Mary Bray. *Another Country: Navigating the Emotional Terrain of Our Elders*. Riverhead Books, 2000.

Sher, Barbara. *It's Only Too Late if You Don't Start Now: How to Create Your Second Life at Any Age*. Dell, 1999.

Sinetar, Marsha. *To Build the Life You Want, Create the Work You Love: The Spiritual Dimension of Entrepreneuring*. St. Martin's, 1996.

Solomon, Marion. *Lean on Me: The Power of Positive Dependency in Intimate Relationships*. Simon & Schuster, 1994.

Tolle, Eckhart. *The Power of Now: A Guide to Spiritual Enlightenment*. Hachette, Australia, 2018.

About the Author

James Nussbaumer has climbed his way out of the deep dark rabbit hole of the prison system and recovers by sharing his story of shifting from darkness to real and true Light.

He states that the experience proves how we all must be "pretty powerful." He further adds, "Let's don't become stuck in darkness when deep down we do know we are truly decent individuals, but as humans in this world we do make mistakes."

When he spotted a spark of light in his thought process it became luminous and brighter as at the same time darkness began fading away. James has proved to his many readers worldwide that in prison he finally realized there must be a way to apply the mental power of this Light to create a much more positive and constructive way to live.

His books continue to arrive onto the scene about the story of humankind and our concentration on behavior. All of the things that frighten us occur in a world of illusion, a collective dream we call life. A miracle is not a rearrangement of the figures in the dream of life, but an awakening from that dream.

James, a former financial advisor for over 25 years speaks

everywhere about his career crash, and welcomes the questions and concerns of truth seekers around the globe about bringing forth miracles into their lives.

He adds that, the miracle is about seeking out a practical goal and a return to inner peace. We're not wishing for something outside us to grant us our life dream, but rather for something within us all to be free and have your life dream be a reality.

Mr. Nussbaumer looks forward to meeting so many of his readers while promoting the series today in your town, at an event, or online, which he says, "This sets him physically and spiritually free."

James lives in Massillon, Ohio, and calls Palm Harbor, FL his second home. He has three daughters and four grandchildren. When you get to know him, you will find that he enjoys the idea of, "Inner Freedom being everything."

Books by James Nussbaumer

Master of Everything
Published by: Ozark Mountain Publishing

Mastering Your Own Spiritual Freedom
Published by: Ozark Mountain Publishing

And Then I Knew My Abundance
Published by: Ozark Mountain Publishing

Living Your Dream, Nit Someone Else's
Published by: Ozark Mountain Publishing

For more information about any of the above titles, soon to be
released
titles, or other items in our catalog, write, phone or visit our website:
Ozark Mountain Publishing, Inc.
PO Box 754, Huntsville, AR 72740
479-738-2348/800-935-0045
www.ozarkmt.com

For more information about any of the titles published by Ozark Mountain Publishing, Inc., soon to be released titles, or other items in our catalog, write, phone or visit our website:

Ozark Mountain Publishing, Inc.

PO Box 754

Huntsville, AR 72740

479-738-2348/800-935-0045

www.ozarkmt.com

Other Books by Ozark Mountain Publishing, Inc.

Dolores Cannon
A Soul Remembers Hiroshima
Between Death and Life
Conversations with Nostradamus,
    Volume I, II, III
The Convoluted Universe -Book One,
    Two, Three, Four, Five
The Custodians
Five Lives Remembered
Jesus and the Essenes
Keepers of the Garden
Legacy from the Stars
The Legend of Starcrash
The Search for Hidden Sacred
    Knowledge
They Walked with Jesus
The Three Waves of Volunteers and
    the New Earth
A Very Special Friend
Horns of the Goddess
Aron Abrahamsen
Holiday in Heaven
James Ream Adams
Little Steps
Justine Alessi & M. E. McMillan
Rebirth of the Oracle
Kathryn Andries
Time: The Second Secret
Cat Baldwin
Divine Gifts of Healing
The Forgiveness Workshop
Penny Barron
The Oracle of UR
P.E. Berg & Amanda Hemmingsen
The Birthmark Scar
Dan Bird
Finding Your Way in the Spiritual Age
Waking Up in the Spiritual Age
Julia Cannon
Soul Speak – The Language of Your
    Body
Ronald Chapman
Seeing True
Jack Churchward
Lifting the Veil on the Lost

Continent of Mu
The Stone Tablets of Mu
Patrick De Haan
The Alien Handbook
Paulinne Delcour-Min
Spiritual Gold
Holly Ice
Divine Fire
Joanne DiMaggio
Edgar Cayce and the Unfulfilled Destiny
    of Thomas Jefferson Reborn
Anthony DeNino
The Power of Giving and Gratitude
Paul Fisher
Like A River To The Sea
Carolyn Greer Daly
Opening to Fullness of Spirit
Anita Holmes
Twidders
Aaron Hoopes
Reconnecting to the Earth
Patricia Irvine
In Light and In Shade
Kevin Killen
Ghosts and Me
Susan Urbanek Linville
Blessing from Agnes
Donna Lynn
From Fear to Love
Curt Melliger
Heaven Here on Earth
Where the Weeds Grow
Henry Michaelson
And Jesus Said – A Conversation
Andy Myers
Not Your Average Angel Book
Holly Nadler
The Hobo Diaries
Guy Needler
Avoiding Karma
Beyond the Source – Book 1, Book 2 The
History of God
The Origin Speaks

For more information about any of the above titles, soon to be released titles,
or other items in our catalog, write, phone or visit our website:
PO Box 754, Huntsville, AR 72740|479-738-2348/800-935-0045|www.ozarkmt.com

Other Books by Ozark Mountain Publishing, Inc.

The Anne Dialogues
The Curators
Psycho Spiritual Healing
James Nussbaumer
And Then I Knew My Abundance
The Master of Everything
Mastering Your Own Spiritual Freedom
Living Your Dram, Not Someone Else's
Each of You
Sherry O'Brian
Peaks and Valley's
Gabrielle Orr
Akashic Records: One True Love
Let Miracles Happen
Nikki Pattillo
Children of the Stars
A Golden Compass
Victoria Pendragon
Sleep Magic
The Sleeping Phoenix
Being In A Body
Alexander Quinn
Starseeds What's It All About
Charmian Redwood
A New Earth Rising
Coming Home to Lemuria
Richard Rowe
Imagining the Unimaginable
Exploring the Divine Library
Garnet Schulhauser
Dancing on a Stamp
Dancing Forever with Spirit
Dance of Heavenly Bliss
Dance of Eternal Rapture
Dancing with Angels in Heaven
Manuella Stoerzer
Headless Chicken
Annie Stillwater Gray
Education of a Guardian Angel
The Dawn Book
Work of a Guardian Angel
Joys of a Guardian Angel

Blair Styra
Don't Change the Channel
Who Catharted
Natalie Sudman
Application of Impossible Things
L.R. Sumpter
Judy's Story
The Old is New
We Are the Creators
Artur Tradevosyan
Croton
Croton II
Jim Thomas
Tales from the Trance
Jolene and Jason Tierney
A Quest of Transcendence
Paul Travers
Dancing with the Mountains
Nicholas Vesey
Living the Life-Force
Dennis Wheatley/ Maria Wheatley
The Essential Dowsing Guide
Maria Wheatley
Druidic Soul Star Astrology
Sherry Wilde
The Forgotten Promise
Lyn Willmott
A Small Book of Comfort
Beyond all Boundaries Book 1
Beyond all Boundaries Book 2
Beyond all Boundaries Book 3
Stuart Wilson & Joanna Prentis
Atlantis and the New Consciousness
Beyond Limitations
The Essenes -Children of the Light
The Magdalene Version
Power of the Magdalene
Sally Wolf
Life of a Military Psychologist

For more information about any of the above titles, soon to be released titles,
or other items in our catalog, write, phone or visit our website:
PO Box 754, Huntsville, AR 72740|479-738-2348/800-935-0045|www.ozarkmt.com